Giuseppe Verdi

Macbeth

OPERA STUDY GUIDE

AND

LIBRETTO

OPERA CLASSICS LIBRARY™

Translated and Edited by Burton D. Fisher
Principal lecturer, *Opera Journeys Lecture Series*

Opera Journeys Publishing™/Boca Raton, Florida

Opera Journeys™ Mini Guide Series

Opera Classics Library™ Series

Opera Journeys™ Libretto Series

A History of Opera:
Milestones and Metamorphoses

Mozart's Da Ponte Operas

PUCCINI COMPANION

Verdi Companion: 27 Opera Study Guide

Over 125 GUIDES & LIBRETTI AVAILABLE: Print or Ebook

•The Abduction from the Seraglio •Adriana Lecouvreur •L'Africaine •Aida
•Andrea Chénier •Anna Bolena •Ariadne auf Naxos •Armida •Attila
•The Ballad of Baby Doe •The Barber of Seville •Duke Bluebeard's Castle
•La Bohème •Boris Godunov •Candide •Capriccio •Carmen
•Cavalleria Rusticana •Cendrillon •La Cenerentola •La Clemenza di Tito
•Le Comte Ory •Così fan tutte •The Crucible •La Damnation de Faust
•The Death of Klinghoffer •Doctor Atomic •Don Carlo •Don Giovanni
•Don Pasquale •La Donna del Lago •The Elixir of Love •Elektra •Ernani
•Eugene Onegin •Exploring Wagner's Ring •Falstaff •La Fanciulla del West
•Faust •La Fille du Régiment •Fidelio •Die Fledermaus •The Flying Dutchman
•Die Frau ohne Schatten •Der Freischütz •Gianni Schicchi •La Gioconda
•Hamlet •Hansel and Gretel •Henry VIII •Iolanta •L'Italiana in Algeri
•Les Huguenots •Iphigénie en Tauride •Julius Caesar •Lakmé •Lohengrin
•Lucia di Lammermoor •Macbeth •Madama Butterfly •The Magic Flute
•The Makropolis Case •Manon •Manon Lescaut •Maria Stuarda
•The Marriage of Figaro •A Masked Ball •Die Meistersinger •The Mikado
•Nabucco •Nixon in China •Norma •Of Mice and Men •Orfeo ed Euridice
•Otello •I Pagliacci •Parsifal •The Pearl Fishers •Pelléas et Mélisande
•Porgy and Bess •Prince Igor •I Puritani •The Queen of Spades
•The Rake's Progress •The Rape of Lucretia •The Rhinegold •Rigoletto
•The Ring of the Nibelung •Roberto Devereaux •Rodalinda •Roméo et Juliette
•La Rondine •Der Rosenkavalier •Rusalka •Salome •Samson and Delilah
•Show Boat •Siegfried •Simon Boccanegra •La Sonnambula •Suor Angelica
•Susannah •Il Tabarro •The Tales of Hoffmann •Tannhäuser •Thaïs •Tosca
•La Traviata •Tristan and Isolde •Il Trittico •Les Troyens •Il Trovatore
•Turandot •The Valkyrie •Werther •West Side Story •Wozzeck

WWW.OPERAJOURNEYS.COM

Contents

WEB SITE: www.operajourneys.com   E MAIL: operaj@bellsouth.net

Prelude
OPERA CLASSICS LIBRARY
Macbeth
OPERA STUDY GUIDE AND LIBRETTO

Verdi's *Macbeth* represents a flowering of the composer's musico-dramatic genius. In this opera, Verdi integrated the power of Shakespeare's words with music that conveys profound passion. *Macbeth* is a hallmark of Italian opera, in which the inherent human conflict becomes intensified by the emotive power of the music.

OPERA CLASSICS LIBRARY explores the greatness and magic of Verdi's ingenious 10th opera. The *Commentary and Analysis* offers pertinent biographical information about Verdi, his mind-set at the time of *Macbeth*'s composition, the ingenious musical inventions he injected into this opera, its premiere and performance history, and insightful story and character analysis.

The text also contains a *Brief Story Synopsis, Principal Characters in Macbeth,* and a *Story Narrative with Music Highlight Examples,* the latter containing original music transcriptions that are interspersed appropriately within the story's dramatic exposition. In addition, the text includes a *Dictionary of Opera and Musical Terms.*

The *Libretto* has been newly translated by the Opera Journeys staff with specific emphasis on retaining a literal translation, but also with the objective to provide a faithful translation in modern and contemporary English; in this way, the substance of the drama becomes more intelligible. To enhance educational and study objectives, the *Libretto* also contains music highlight examples interspersed within the flow of the drama.

The opera art form is the sum of many artistic expressions: theatrical drama, music, scenery, poetry, dance, acting and gesture. In opera, it is the composer who is the dramatist, using the power of his music to express intense, human conflicts. Words evoke thought, but music provokes feelings; opera's sublime fusion of words, music and all the theatrical arts provide powerful theater, an impact on one's sensibilities that can reach into the very depths of the human soul.

Verdi's *Macbeth,* a crown jewel of his glorious operatic inventions, remains a masterpiece of musico-dramatic theater, a tribute to the evolution of the art form as well as to its ingenious composer.

Burton D. Fisher
Editor
OPERA CLASSICS LIBRARY

Macbeth

Opera in Italian in four acts

Music

by

Giuseppe Verdi

Libretto byFrancesco Maria Piave,

after Shakespeare's *Macbeth*, Globe Theater, London (1605)

Premiere: Teatro della Pergola, Florence, Italy,

March 1847 (Revised in 1865)

Macbeth

Opera in Italian in four acts

Music

by

Giuseppe Verdi

Libretto byFrancesco Maria Piave,

after Shakespeare's *Macbeth,* Globe Theater, London (1605)

Premiere: Teatro della Pergola, Florence, Italy, March 1847

Revised in 1865

Commentary and Analysis

Giuseppe Verdi began his opera composing career in 1839, a time when the styles and techniques of Italian opera, which had dominated the art form for over two centuries, were on the verge of ceding their supremacy. Many believed that opera had become stilted, old fashioned, and had even degenerated: Wagner's primary goal in his crusade at mid-century was to rescue opera from the decadence of Italian opera conventions.

Verdi's most immediate operatic guidelines evolved from the *primo ottocento,* a term loosely defining Italian music and opera during the first half of the 19th century. Verdi's immediate predecessors, Rossini, Bellini, and Donizetti, had dominated the early Romantic period and the *bel canto,* literally, the era of "beautiful singing, or "beautiful song."

Rossini was the architect who established the models for opera styles and conventions: he revitalized and refashioned the *opera buffa* (comic) and *opera seria* (serious) genres, and established the grammar and structural framework which every composer dutifully followed. In particular, Bellini and Donizetti initially emulated Rossini before they developed their own specific musical signatures. And quite naturally, Verdi was an heir to those traditions, his early operas adhering religiously to the conventions of *bel canto* structure and architecture. *Macbeth,* Verdi's seventh opera, was opera composed in the *bel canto* traditions and structural conventions of the Romantic period.

In the *bel canto* era, opera was a singer's medium, a venue providing an arena in which to display the vocal arts and feats of vocal acrobatics. Opera was rarely sung drama: its literary and dramatic values became secondary to singing and rarely if ever bore any organic relationship or unity with its underlying music. The emphasis on voice, which peaked during the *bel canto* era, was a legacy that traced back to 18th century modes in which the singer and his vocal talents, not the composer as the musical dramatist, dominated the art form. As a result, opera composers were obliged to cater to vocal superstars who became, in effect, their austere clients.

Verdi's early musical language and techniques dutifully followed those of his predecessors: his early operas were composed in the traditions of the *bel canto* era, in which the vocal art remained primary: the orchestra was generally relegated to the secondary role of accompanist, "number" operas were integrated with recitative, and architecturally, all of the standard structural conventions were utilized; *cavatinas* (relatively simple single-part arias), *cabalettas* (generally two-part arias with fast and slow sections), and *strettas* (fast tempo finales of arias, duets, or ensembles).

But for Verdi, the opera art form was a forum in which he could expound his idealism: he would use his art form like a priest and teach morality. And through opera, he would convey profound human passions by combining the potency words with the emotive power of music. Temperamentally, Verdi was a son of the Enlightenment. He was an idealist who possessed a noble conception of humanity that abominated absolute power and deified civil liberty: his lifelong manifesto became a passionate crusade against every form of tyranny whether social, political, or ecclesiastical. During his first creative period, 1839 – 1850, his mission was a profound emotional commitment to Italy's liberation from foreign oppression and tyranny: he composed 16 operas during that period, each embedded with symbolism, allegory, and metaphor; Verdi's operatic pen provided his nation's anthems for freedom.

At the age of 26, his first opera, *Oberto* (1839), was produced at La Scala, Milan. The opera was an acclaimed success, but more importantly, it nurtured optimism and expectation that finally, an Italian opera composer had appeared to revive their then decaying traditions. Unfortunately, his second opera, the comedy, *Un Giorno di Regno* (1840), proved a disastrous failure. But in his third opera, *Nabucco* (1842), Verdi's inventive melodic genius came to the fore: *Nabucco* was saturated with what eventually became the composer's musical trademark; broad, grandiose, and tuneful melodies.

From *Nabucco* onward, his operas became more unified in their integration of text and music; his characterizations began to possess an intense depth and express profound human values; and his music became injected with powerful psychological and emotional feeling: Verdi's goal was to use his music to bypass surface emotion and superficiality, an art form that would penetrate the soul of humanity.

Nabucco was followed with one success after another: *I Lombardi* (1843); *Ernani* (1844); *I Due Foscari* (1844); *Giovanna d'Arco* (1845); *Alzira* (1845); *Attila* (1846); *Macbeth* (1847); *I Masnadieri* (1847); *Il Corsaro* (1848); *La Battaglia di Legnano* (1849); *Luisa Miller* (1849); and *Stiffelio* (1850).

Beginning in 1851, Verdi's "middle period," his creative art began to flower into a new maturity: he began to composed what have become some of the best loved works ever written for the operatic stage; *Rigoletto* (1851); *Il Trovatore* (1853); *La Traviata* (1853); *I Vespri Siciliani* (1855); *Simon Boccanegra* (1857); *Aroldo* (1857); *Un Ballo in Maschera* (1859); *La Forza del Destino* (1862); *Don Carlos* (1867); and *Aïda* (1871).

As Verdi approached the twilight of his illustrious and prolific operatic career, he confounded the strictures of time and nature: he should have been relishing his "golden years," a time when the fires of ambition were supposed to extinguish, and a time when he was supposed to become a spectator in life's show rather than its star. Nevertheless, the great opera composer epitomized the words of Robert Browning's Rabbi Ben Ezra: "Grow old along with me. The best is yet to be."

Consequently, Verdi overturned life's equation and transformed his old age into glory: "The best is yet to be" became his last two operatic masterpieces, inviolable proof of his continued advance toward greater dramatic integration between text and music, and ultimately, his transformation of opera into music drama.

Those last operas, *Otello* (1887), and *Falstaff* (1893), are considered by many to be the greatest Italian music dramas ever composed, both written respectively at the ages of 74 and 80. Verdi eventually composed 28 operas during his illustrious career, dying in 1901 at the age of 88.

William Shakespeare's *Macbeth*, a tragedy in five acts, was first performed at the Globe Theatre, London, in 1605. The play was inspired by fears emanating from the rebellious Gunpowder Plot in 1605: its story focused on regicide and was intended to awaken suspicion in the new king, James I. In its day, *Macbeth* was a tremendous success, and likewise, it remains one of the most frequently performed of Shakespeare's plays. It is the shortest of Shakespeare's high tragedies, one-half as long as *Hamlet*, nevertheless, it is a rapid-fire drama possessing an almost ruthless economy of words, and like *Othello,* containing no diversions or subplots.

The time-frame of the *Macbeth* drama is the years 1040-1057. The historical Macbeth was a local chieftain in the province of Moray in northern Scotland. Macbeth and his cousin, Duncan, derived their rights to the crown through their mothers, but Macbeth attained the throne in 1040 after killing King Duncan in a battle near Elgin: Shakespeare controverted historical fact and presented King Duncan murdered by Macbeth in his bed.

Scotland's civil wars for power continued unabated, but in 1045, Macbeth secured his throne by triumphing over a rebel army near Dunkeld, the modern Tayside region, which suggest Shakespeare's references to Birnam Wood, which is a village near Dunkeld. In 1046, Siward, Earl of Northumbria, unsuccessfully attempted to dethrone Macbeth in favor of Malcolm, eldest son of Duncan I: in 1054, Siward forced Macbeth to yield part of southern Scotland to Malcolm. Three years later, Macbeth was killed in battle by Malcolm, who had been assisted by the English armies.

Macbeth was buried on the island of Iona, traditionally a cemetery for lawful kings but not usurpers. His followers later attempted to install his stepson, Lulach, as king, but Lulach was killed in 1058, and Malcolm III became the supreme ruler of Scotland.

Shakespeare's contemporary rival, Ben Johnson, praised him as a writer "not of an age, but for all time," a universal genius and literary high priest who invented through his dramas, a secular scripture from which we derive much of our language, much of our psychology, and much of our mythology.

It has been said that Shakespeare, through his dramas, invented the human: his works hold a mirror up to humanity which lays bare its soul. His character inventions take human nature to its limits and have become truthful representations of the human experience: Hamlet, Falstaff, Iago, and Cleopatra; it is through those characterizations that one turns inward and discovers new modes of awareness and consciousness. Shakespeare's ultimate legacy is that for four centuries, his plays have become the wheel of our lives, teaching us through their universal themes, whether we are fools of time, of love, of fortune, or even of ourselves.

Giuseppe Verdi had a life-long veneration for Shakespeare, his singular and most popular source of literary inspiration, far more profound to him than the playwrights Goldoni, Goethe, Schiller, Hugo, and Racine. Verdi said of Shakespeare: "He is a favorite poet of mine whom I have had in my hands from earliest youth and whom I read and reread constantly."

The desire to compose operas based on Shakespeare's dramas was a leitmotif threading though Verdi's entire career. He dreamed of bringing *Hamlet* and *King Lear* to the operatic stage: both were ambitious projects that never reached fruition. In particular, *King Lear's* intricacy and bold extremities represented an imposing deterrent. Even late in his career, Boito submitted a sketch to him after the success of *Otello*, but he hesitated, considering himself too old to undertake what he deemed a monumental challenge.

In 1847, the 34 year old Verdi received a commission from the Teatro della Pergola in Florence to compose an opera for the Carnival or Lenten season. Verdi was nearing completion of *I Masnadieri* "The Robbers," but its leading role was dependent on a tenor and none was available: he turned to Shakespeare's *Macbeth,* an opera that he had conceived without a tenor lead.

In opera, the composer of music, not the playwright, is the dramatist of the story. Verdi had been continually evolving and refining his musico-dramatic techniques, and technically and temperamentally, he was ready for the emotional and dramatic scope of this Shakespearean work. An opera based on Verdi's favorite dramatist was an inevitability: *Macbeth*, his seventh opera, became the first of his three music dramas based on Shakespeare's plays; *Otello* (1887) and *Falstaff* (1893) belong to the last phase of his career

Shakespearean plots are saturated with extravagant passions that are well-suited to the opera medium. Themes of love dominate both his tragedies and comedies, as well as classic confrontations and universal themes involving hate, jealousy, and revenge. Dramatically, *Macbeth* possesses consummate power: it is one of the best constructed and most vividly theatrical of all of Shakespeare's dramas; its conflicts and tensions essentially progress with no episodes that fail to bear on the central action; and all of its action is focused toward its dramatic core and purpose.

In deference to Shakespeare, Verdi resolved to be as faithful as possible to the original play. He selected as his librettist, Francesco Maria Piave, the poet who had collaborated with him on his recent successes, *Ernani* (1844) and *I Due Foscari* (1844), and would eventually become his librettist for nine of his operas.

Verdi wrote to Piave about *Macbeth*: "This tragedy is one of the greatest creations of man! If we can't do something great with it let's at least try to do something different…" Verdi and Piave faced that eternal challenge inherent in converting Shakespeare to the lyric stage: they had to retain the dramatic essence of the original drama while stripping the drama of its verbal intricacies: much of its word-play, eloquent speech, and poetic language are intrinsically not easily transformed into music theater, a possible reason that many operatic adaptations of Shakespeare are far removed from their originals. Librettist Arrigo Boito faced that same challenge almost a half century later when he reduced *Othello's* monumental 3500 lines to 700 lines for Verdi's *Otello.*

Composer and librettist battled vigorously, Verdi at times bullying his librettist with strict instructions about the sequence of scenes and details of characterizations, and even occasionally supplying Piave with his own prose versions of certain sections. Even Verdi's friend, Andrea Maffei, a renowned Shakespearean and collaborator with Verdi on the libretto of *I Masnadieri*, retouched certain passages and contributed to the final *Macbeth* scenario.

The premiere of *Macbeth* in 1847 was a sensational critical success: the cheering audience expressed fanatical enthusiasm, and the composer was forced to take 25 bows. In retrospect, Verdi was so pleased with the opera that he considered it worthy of dedication to Antonio Barezzi: his expression of gratitude to the man who had been his benefactor, surrogate father, and former father-in-law.

However, in 1865, eighteen years after its premiere, Verdi revised and added material to *Macbeth* for a Parisian production: additions included Lady Macbeth's stirring sunset song, *La luce langue*; the vengeance duet for Macbeth and Lady Macbeth, *Ora di morte*; Macbeth's death scene, *Inno di vittoria;* the concluding choruses, *Patria oppressa* and the thanksgiving chorus; and a ballet, forbidden in the original score because the opera had been commissioned for the Lenten season

The Parisian critics were cool and even disapproved of the revised opera. Verdi was puzzled and disappointed. Some critics condemned him as neither knowing nor understanding Shakespeare. The composer responded: "I may not have rendered *Macbeth* well, but that I do not know, do not understand and feel Shakespeare, no by heaven, no!…" Nevertheless, it is the revised Paris version of *Macbeth* which is generally performed in contemporary times.

Macbeth is a complex personality whose terrifying evil dominates the dramatic action in the story: his demonic persona soars and plummets with each new situation, inspiring him to horrifying and terrifying acts. Cold-blooded murder becomes his natural, customary, and characteristic behavior: his victims become those who interfere with his obsession and ambition for power; King Duncan, Banquo, Lady Macduff, and her children.

In Shakespeare's high tragedies, the characterization of Hamlet and King Lear contain scope and depth, Othello a painfulness, and Antony and Cleopatra, a world without end. In *Macbeth,* the core of the drama concerns unknown fears, all of which evolve from Macbeth's imagination. His fears lead him to hallucinations and imaginings, and then into a nihilistic abyss. However, Macbeth is not a fiendish Iago, confident and delighting in his wickedness, but rather, an insecure demon whose internal conflicts transform his soul into torment and agony.

Macbeth surrenders to his imagination, ultimately evolving into his misery, fear, and evil actions: the extraordinary and enormous power of fantasy engulfs him in phantasmagoria and witchcraft, all of which alter reality and events. He suffers intensely as each stage of his diabolical terror advances: he becomes a victim of compulsion that he cannot control.

At the outset of the play, Macbeth is a brave and respected soldier, a trusted general in King Duncan's army. He becomes overcome by ambition, his motivation to change the course of Scotland's succession: he becomes susceptible and vulnerable, ultimately the victim of the Weird Sisters' prophesies (Verdi's Witches), and then the goading and stirring of Lady Macbeth.

Shakespeare does not portray the Macbeths as Machiavellian exaggerations, or even as power-obsessed sadists: their lust and fiery ambition for the throne is simply that they become victims of desire. However, once they achieve their goals, they are compelled to protect their crown: childless and without heirs from their own union, their only alternative is force and terror; scruples are nonexistent.

Macbeth is a drama which portrays a journey into the darkness deep within an evil soul, a primordial world that has become saturated with murder, horror, and terror; a world in which Macbeth's imagination and phantasmagoria transform into ceaseless bloodshed. In Macbeth's world, the blood spilled in the murders of Banquo and Duncan become his natural order. In the aftermath of confronting Banquo's ghost, overcome by his imagination, Macbeth faces the horror of his inner soul: "It will have blood, they say: blood will have blood."

Lady Macbeth is a strong and calculating woman, determined to see her husband relinquish his "milk of human kindness" in order that he fulfill the ambitions she envisions for both of them. She taunts her husband, urges him onward, and succeeds in goading him to murder King Duncan: ironically, she herself cannot slay the sleeping Duncan because the good king resembles her father in his slumber.

When Macbeth imagines Banquo's ghost, Lady Macbeth intervenes to announce that Macbeth is prone to seizures: "My Lord is often thus/ And hath been from his youth." But Macbeth has surrendered to visionary fits that have overcome him and led him out of control: irrational forces and unknown images have overwhelmed and contaminated him; Lady Macbeth is impotent and cannot control his conscience.

Nevertheless, Lady Macbeth and Macbeth are profoundly in love with each other, ironically perhaps, the most happily married couple in Shakespeare's canon. Their mutual passion depends on their dream of shared greatness: they are motivated by desire, ambition, and power.

But the Macbeths are childless and have no heirs. Lady Macbeth speaks of having nursed a child, presumably her own, but the child is now dead. Macbeth, her second husband, urges her to conceive male children, but they cannot: there is pathos in Lady Macbeth's famous exclamation "To bed." In their madness, murder has become their sole mode of sexual expression. Freud suggested that childlessness became the Macbeths' haunting curse: unable to beget children, they slaughter children in revenge. For Macbeth, that genocide represents his overwhelming need to prove his manhood to his wife: he is, therefore, motivated to destroy Macduff's children, and stimulated to fiercely seek to murder Fleance, Banquo's son.

Lady Macbeth, unequivocally the most powerful character in the drama, is removed from Shakespeare's stage after Act III, Scene iv. She only returns briefly in her state of madness at the start of Act V: she is conquered by inner demons as she glides through her sleepwalking scene, a grotesque woman of undaunted evil calculation who has become transformed into a guilty soul and now despairingly tries to wash invisible blood from her hands as she follows her path into madness and suicide.

Nietzsche reflected on *Macbeth* in *Daybreak* (1881), suggesting that it is erroneous to conclude that Shakespeare's theater has a moral purpose intended to repel man from the evil of ambition. Nietzsche's hypothesis: man is by nature possessed by raging ambitions, which are a glorious end in themselves: man beholds those images joyfully, thwarted only when his passions perish. In Nietzsche's context, *Tristan and Isolde* are not preaching against adultery when they both perish from it: they are embracing it.

In a Judeo-Christian context, *Macbeth* deals with the immorality of evil. However, Shakespeare does not endow *Macbeth* with theological relevance: *Macbeth* is a primordial "man of blood," who, like Hamlet, Lear, and Otello, possesses a universal villainy that transcends Biblical strictures. Shakespeare traditionally evades or blurs Christian values: he is not a devotional dramatist, and he wrote no holy sonnets exposing the divine, or the path to redemption of the soul. Shakespeare presents pragmatic nihilism, an instinctive form of survival rather than a theological supernaturalism: Shakespeare's high tragedies provide no spiritual comfort.

Macbeth is a primordial hunter of men who displays a shocking and energetic vitality for death, violence, and murder. In *Macbeth,* there is no spiritual truth, and God is exiled from his soul: Macbeth rules in a cosmological emptiness where a divine being is lost, too far away to be summoned. In Shakespeare's world, there is only grief and death, but no spiritual solace. Macbeth's crimes are against nature and humanity, not repaired or restored by the social order, or through redeeming grace, expiation, or forgiveness. Time notoriously dominates *Macbeth,* not Christian time with its linear paths to eternal salvation, but devouring time in which death is the nihilistic finality: death and time all integrate and become Macbeth's evil soul.

The Weird Sisters become Macbeth's will and destiny. They become his imagination and his alter ego that overpower his mind, but his ambitions were merely brewing and awaiting their elevation to consciousness: after the Witches, Macbeth was well prepared for Lady Macbeth's greater temptations and unsanctified violence.

Macbeth transforms into a ferocious killing machine; his terror and tyranny manifesting themselves in a slaughterhouse reeking with blood. Macduff becomes Macbeth's nemesis, his birth by cesarean section making him the fulfillment of the Weird Sisters' prophecy: no man of woman born will slay Macbeth; Macduff was "untimely ripped" from his mother's womb. Macbeth's fear of Macduff propels him to his horrifying reign of terror: he slaughters Macduff's wife, children, and servants.

However, Macbeth's bloody deeds gnaw at him and threaten him in his nightmares. Nightmares become the true plot of the drama: his subconscious participates in dreadfulness, and he allows it to rise to horrible imaginings. Samuel Johnson aptly evaluated the essence of the *Macbeth* drama: "the dangerous prevalence of the imagination." *Macbeth* is about nihilism, saturated with the fullness of sound and fury: it portrays the darkness and evil lying within the human soul.

Verdi's *Macbeth* is a music drama in which the emotive power of his music severely influences the text: the opera does not contain the exaggerated emotions and stereotypical characterizations of melodrama. In *Macbeth*, Verdi provided intense dramatic expression in a broad and sweeping musical style, at the same time, maintaining an extraordinary dramatic pace and swiftness by keeping recitative short and concise, and connecting set numbers with cohesive transitions. His music captures the eerie bleakness of Shakespeare's play in a highly charged dramatic tone painting that is equally sustained by psychologically penetrating characterizations.

Opera is an art form for voices: in opera, the voice is the inherent keystone for characterization. At the time of *Macbeth,* Verdi developed his most singular voice innovation: the "high baritone," a unique voice-type capable of providing sharp and distinctive characterization. The "high baritone" is a true baritone voice rather than a raised bass or dark tenor: it extends its range and moves comfortably higher than the bass or traditional baritone, ultimately reaching an A (above middle C).

The "high baritone" represented the core of Verdi's new musico-dramatic art: a masculine voice which could reach out to encompass an entire spectrum of emotion and character. This new "high baritone" voice became the embodiment of force from which Verdi could bring other voices into sharp contrast and focus. In *Ernani* (Verdi's fifth opera, 1844), and likewise in *Macbeth,* the musico-dramatic force derives from the contrast of vocal archetypes. Verdi was now able to clearly delineate specific character qualities through the male voice: the tenor would possess an ardent, lyrical, and despairing sound; the bass would convey a darkness and inflexibility in tone; and the "new baritone," a heretofore unknown luster and quality. The "new baritone" became a dynamo of vocal energy that was capable of expressing every color within the emotional spectrum. With his "new baritone," Verdi was able to portray the dramatic essence of Macbeth's character, the inherent qualities of the voice enabling him to truthfully sculpt Macbeth's demonic and volcanic energy.

Shakespeare portrays Macbeth as a man obsessed by conflict, tension, and villainy. Verdi used his new "high baritone" to portray a man suffering from his emotional and psychological disasters and his inner turmoil. When the Witches predict the crown for Macbeth, Verdi adroitly uses the qualities of the "high baritone" voice to focus on Macbeth's terror and bewilderment.

In *Macbeth,* the villain's insanity results from his hallucinations and delirium, grist for the operatic mill where composers traditionally find their muse and inspiration. Some classic operatic characters, who are punished by madness and self-destruct through guilt for their misdeeds, are Nabucco, Macbeth, Boris Godunov, Wozzeck, and Peter Grimes. Verdi dutifully and ingeniously captures that magical operatic moment of Macbeth's madness when he erupts into hysteria after his failure to control the illusion of Banquo's ghost and wonders, "Can the tomb give up the murdered?" Lady Macbeth adds the final outrage as her husband cowers before the ghost: she demands "Are you a man?" Verdi's music magnificently reaches into the Macbeths inner souls.

Nevertheless, vocally, Verdi made Lady Macbeth perhaps the most dominant figure in his opera. She, like her predecessor, Abigaile in *Nabucco,* is a dramatic soprano whose character is sharply and extravagantly drawn musically: these dramatic sopranos became the female equivalent of Verdi's "new baritone" power. Lady Macbeth is allotted some of the best, most absorbing dramatic pages of Verdi's score: her aria, *La luce langue,* "The light falls," a brilliant expression of conflicts and tensions, of fear and exultation; her jolly *brindisi;* and the stupendous Sleepwalking episode for which a Verdi biographer commented that "the composer rises to the level of the poet and gives the full equivalent in music of the spoken word."

In *Macbeth,* Verdi provided a super-charged drama with ingenious melodic inventions. The score is saturated with broad and arching lyric phrases, melodies that contain a sweeping, forward thrust, duets that contain a remarkably wide range of expression and contrast, and large ensembles which express a succession of intense dramatic ideas.

Macbeth contains a taut, fast moving libretto that gathers tension and momentum as it takes the plot racing along clearly and decisively from climax to climax. Shakespeare's plot may have benefited from its transformation into an opera: the opera's text moves tensely and directly toward the drama's conclusion.

Verdi's art was continually evolving and maturing: he would eventually transform existing Italian operatic conventions but did not overturn them. *Macbeth* is an enthralling work in which the master reached beyond the confines of his contemporary Italian opera conventions and traditions: there is much *bel canto* in the score, and structurally, many existing traditions and conventions are followed *de rigeur.* Nevertheless, in *Macbeth,* Verdi provided many glimpses of a new freedom in operatic expression that would very quickly flower in his subsequent operas.

Macbeth became a springboard for Verdi to bring more intense and profound passions to the operatic stage: nevertheless, it is an opera with powerful drama and unrivalled musical beauty, a worthy tribute to his favorite poetic inspiration: William Shakespeare.

Principal Characters in Macbeth

Macbeth, Thane of Glamis and a Scottish general in the army of King Duncan	Baritone
Lady Macbeth, his wife	Soprano
Banquo (Banco), a Scottish general	Bass
Duncan, King of Scotland	Tenor
Malcolm, Duncan's son	Tenor
Macduff, a nobleman	Tenor
An assassin	Baritone
Lady-in-Waiting to Lady Macbeth, a gentlewoman	Soprano
A Doctor	Bass
Hecate, goddess of night and witchcraft	Dancer

The Three Witches, Nobles, refugees,
Scottish and British Soldiers, Attendants, Apparitions

TIME and PLACE: 11th century, Scotland

Brief Story Synopsis

Verdi's *Macbeth* dutifully mirrors the essence of Shakespeare's tragedy: the powerful drama chronicles the rise and fall of Macbeth and Lady Macbeth and their ultimate destruction resulting from their blind ambition to seize and maintain power in 11th century Scotland.

Banquo and Macbeth, generals serving King Duncan in Scotland's war against England, accidentally encounter the three "Weird Sisters" — Witches who prophesy that Macbeth will become Thane of Cawdor: therefore, next in line as king of Scotland; Banquo's lineage will succeed Macbeth.

Lady Macbeth, consumed by her ambition for power, spurs her husband to kill King Duncan while he spends a night at their castle at Dunsinane. After the King's murder, fearing for their lives, Duncan's son Malcolm flees Scotland: Macbeth becomes king.

Fearing the Witches' prophecy, Macbeth has Banquo assassinated, but his son, Fleance, escapes. Macbeth, in fear and guilt, becomes haunted by visions of Banquo's ghost.

He again seeks the Witches' predictions: they assure him that his power will be secure until Birnam Wood arises against Dunsinane, and that no man "of woman born" shall harm him.

Macbeth learns that Macduff joined Malcolm's rebel army and orders the slaughter of Malcolm's wife and children. His enemies, camouflaged with branches from Birnam Wood, advance on Dunsinane: Macbeth envisions their assault as a fulfillment of the Witches' prophecy.

Lady Macbeth dies, driven to madness by her guilt. Macduff kills Macbeth in battle. It is the final fulfillment of the Witches' prophesy: Macduff was not "of woman born," but "from his mother's womb untimely ripp'd."

Malcolm, Duncan's son, becomes Scotland's king, ending Macbeth's brutal reign of tyranny and terror.

Story Narrative and Music Highlights

Prelude:

The prelude furnishes various musical themes that express grim aspects of the tragedy. The first music portrays the Witches, conveying a shrillness, malevolence, and their demonic character.

A second theme captures music from Lady Macbeth's Act IV *Sleepwalking Scene*; mournful music that suggests the gnawing guilt in the recesses of Lady Macbeth's subconscious.

ACT I – Scene 1: A wooded landscape. A group of three Witches appear amid a storm.

Roars of thunder and flashes of lightning evoke a terrifying atmosphere: a chorus of Witches sing and dance, priding their malevolence, and invoking themselves as children of Satan.

Macbeth and Banquo, Scottish generals returning from a victorious battle against their English foe, accidentally encounter the Witches. The Witches greet Macbeth, now Thane of Glamis, and prophesy that he will soon become Thane of Cawdor, a rank that would place him next in line as king of Scotland.

Witches: Salve, o Macbetto, di Glamis sire!

The Witches' prediction of sudden good fortune seizes Macbeth with fear and anxiety. Banquo, equally stunned, commands the Witches to reveal his future, and they prophesy that he will never be king, but the progenitor of future kings.

The Witches' prophesy becomes fulfilled immediately: a messenger arrives and announces that King Duncan has proclaimed Macbeth the next Thane of Cawdor: his predecessor has been executed for treason, and his lands and title have been assigned to Macbeth.

Macbeth and Banquo, overwhelmed by the sudden events, express their inner sentiments: Macbeth's ambition possesses and overpowers his imagination: he becomes perplexed, anxious, and seized by thoughts of horror and terror; Banquo remains skeptical.

Macbeth: Due vaticini compiuti or sono

The Witches, noting the anxiety of the two men, erupt in triumph: they have planted their evil seeds, and now await the flowering of their malevolence.

Scene 2: A hall in Macbeth's castle.

Lady Macbeth reads a letter from Macbeth in which he describes his meeting with the Witches and their prophesy for his future. She explodes into uncontrollable excitement as she envisions their forthcoming rise to power: she bids Macbeth hurry home so she can incite him with her diabolical plans; for Lady Macbeth, no crime shall thwart her obsessive ambition for power.

Lady Macbeth: Vieni t'afretta

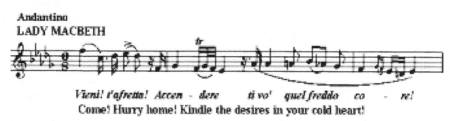

A messenger announces that Macbeth has arrived with King Duncan's entourage: the King plans to spend the night in Macbeth's castle. Lady Macbeth, energized by this sudden opportunity to fulfill her dreams, invokes the powers of darkness as she contemplates the murder of King Duncan.

Lady Macbeth: Or tutti sorgete

King Duncan and his entourage parade briefly before Macbeth and Lady Macbeth, a few gracious words are exchanged, and then the King retires for the night.

In a tense confrontation, Lady Macbeth reveals her diabolical murder plans to her husband, goading him to assassinate King Duncan that very night. Macbeth becomes possessed by fantastic images: he envisions the dagger, and as a night bell sounds, he rushes off to murder Duncan.

Macbeth returns to the awaiting Lady Macbeth, his hands bloody and still holding the dagger. In triumph, he announces *Tutto è finito!*, "All is done!"

In a sinister exchange between husband and wife, Lady Macbeth orders Macbeth to lay the bloody dagger near the guards so that they will appear to be guilty of Duncan's murder. But Macbeth is horrified by his actions and is unable to return to the murder scene. Scornfully, Lady Macbeth seizes the dagger, rushes into the king's chamber, and places the bloody dagger beside his bed.

Loud knocks on the castle gates herald the arrival of Banquo and Macduff. Macbeth, his hands drenched with King Duncan's blood, is led by Lady Macbeth to their quarters to avoid suspicion.

Banquo enters the King's quarters to awaken him and finds him murdered. All are summoned, express their horrified anguish, and then pray for divine guidance for vengeance and justice.

Act II – Scene 1: A room in Macbeth's castle

Malcolm is suspected of Duncan's murder and flees Scotland. Macbeth is now King, but he is apprehensive and insecure of his new power. He becomes tormented by subconscious imaginings and guilt, and fears the Witches' prophesy: Banquo's sons will become the future kings of Scotland. Lady Macbeth persuades Macbeth to murder Banquo and his heirs. With fiercely determination, she urges her husband to be undaunted in his purpose: his resolve must remain firm, never weaken nor fail him; he must murder Banquo so he can fulfill his destiny and glory.

Lady Macbeth: La luce langue

La   lu - ce lan - gue,   il   fa - ro spe - gnesi
THe warm and tender sun will never be extinguished...........

Scene 2: A park near Macbeth's castle

Macbeth's assassins wait in ambush to murder Banquo. Banquo appears with his son, Fleance, and meditates about his fears for his future.

Banquo: Come dal ciel precipita

Co - me dal ciel   pre-ci - pita   l'ombra più sempre oscura!
On this night of reckoning, ghosts of the past confound me!

Assassins murder Banquo, but his son, Fleance, escapes.

Scene 3: The Banquet hall

Scotland's King and Queen, Macbeth and Lady Macbeth, are acclaimed at a banquet. Macbeth summons Lady Macbeth to celebrate and lead the noble guests in a *brindisi*, a drinking song praising happiness and love, and a farewell to anxiety and suffering.

Lady Macbeth: the Brindisi; Si colmi il calice

Si   col - mi il   ca - lice   di   vi - no e - let - to...
I drink to happiness, to love, and laughter!

As the closing strains of the *brindisi* echo, an assassin advises Macbeth that they have murdered Banquo, but unfortunately, his son Fleance escaped.

Macbeth becomes possessed by hallucinations: he alone believes that Banquo's ghost occupies a chair at the banquet table. Macbeth, incoherent and lacking presence of mind, addresses the empty chair. Lady Macbeth tries to discourage and calm him by repeating her *brindisi*, ironically proposing a toast to the health of the absent Banquo. But Macbeth, overcome with terror, cannot erase the vision of Banquo and proceeds to speak to the ghost.

In the confusion, Lady Macbeth tries to assuage the guests, declaring that the dead cannot return to life. However, Macbeth has become possessed by fear and guilt: he is determined to learn his fate and decides to seek the prophesies from the Witches.

Act III: A dark cave. A burning cauldron surrounded by Witches.

In a bizarre display of supernatural imagery, the Witches sing and dance as they hover over a flaming caldron.

Chorus of Witches: Tre volte miagola

Hecate, the goddess of night and witchcraft, appears before them and announces the arrival of King Macbeth: she orders the Witches to answer his questions, and should his composure break down, the spirits must revive and reinvigorate him.

Macbeth pleads with the Witches to predict his destiny. The Witches conjure up a series of apparitions, each preceded by a lightning bolt. The first apparition, the head of an armed warrior, warns Macbeth to beware that Macduff, Thane of Fife, is his mortal enemy. Macbeth acknowledges to the spirit that it confirms his own suspicions, but the next apparition, a bloody child, assures Macbeth that he need fear no man of woman born: Macbeth ecstatically proclaims that he no longer fears Macduff.

Another apparition predicts that Macbeth shall never be vanquished until the forest of Birnam Wood shall rise. Macbeth becomes overjoyed by the news, convinced that he is protected: Birnam Wood's firmly planted trees can never be uprooted.

Macbeth asks the Witches if Banquo's heirs will one day wear the crown of Scotland. Suddenly, the spirits of eight kings pass by: each disappears and is replaced by another apparition. The eighth king is Banquo: he holds a mirror, a symbol indicating that kings will stem from his lineage. Macbeth attacks the apparition of Banquo with his sword, but the apparition, along with the Witches themselves, vanish.

Macbeth, possessed with fear and terror, faints and falls to the ground.

Macbeth: *Fuggi, regal fantasima*

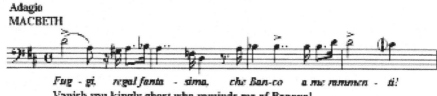

Lady Macbeth arrives and demands to know what Macbeth has learned from the Witches. Macbeth reveals their prophesies: beware of Macduff; that Macbeth shall not die by the hand of one born of woman; that Macbeth's glory shall last until the forest of Birnam Wood shall rise against him; and that Banquo's offspring shall wear the crown.

Lady Macbeth erupts into ferocious outrage. She condemns the Witches' prophesies as lies and frauds, and vows that they will never be fulfilled: anyone opposed to the Macbeths must be destroyed.

Lady Macbeth succeeds in restoring Macbeth's determination and purpose: he decides to demolish Macduff's castle and slay his wife and children; he will find and murder Banquo's son, Fleance. Lady Macbeth prides her valiant husband, who has returned once more to bravery: both unite and swear vengeance on their enemies; Scotland will witness a bloody dawn of destruction: a reign of terror that will secure the Macbeth's power.

Macbeth: *Ora di morte e di vendetta!*

ACT IV – Scene 1: Open country near Birnam Wood on the border of England and Scotland

Refugees from Macbeth's tyranny express their patriotism and sorrow over Scotland's misfortunes: *Patria oppressa,* "Oppressed homeland!"

Macduff, whose wife and children were murdered by Macbeth, laments his agony and grief.

Macduff: Ah, la paterna mano

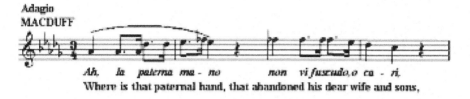

Malcolm arrives with soldiers from England. In preparation for an attack on Macbeth's castle of Dunsinane, he orders his men to camouflage themselves with branches from Birnam Wood's trees.

Scene 2: A Room in Macbeth's castle at Dunsinane.

Lady Macbeth walks in her sleep. Her physician and lady-in- waiting comment about her apparent loss of mind: she is subconsciously consumed with guilt, and in incoherent and disjointed phrases, recalls King Duncan's murder, all the while, rubbing imaginary blood from her hands.

Lady Macbeth: Una macchia

In another part of the castle, Macbeth condemns the traitors who have rebelled against him. He is haunted by the Witches' prophesies, but is undaunted in his determination to defeat his enemies and secure his power.

In a moment of introspection, Macbeth becomes possessed by the death and destruction he has fomented: he laments his legacy; no tears will fall on his death, only the thunder of curses from the oppressed. A woman announces that Lady Macbeth died: Macbeth shows neither indifference nor disdain; for him, the fury of life has resolved into nothingness.

Macbeth's soldiers announce that Birnam wood moves toward Dunsiname. Macbeth secures his armor, and goes off to battle.

Scene 3: A battlefield outside Dunsinane Castle.

Malcolm, Macduff, and English soldiers, camouflaged with branches from Birnam Wood, advance on Macbeth's castle. Macduff confronts Macbeth, and just as he is about to slay him, Macbeth proclaims that no one born of woman can strike him dead. Macduff contradicts him, claiming that he was not born of woman but ripped untimely from the womb. Macbeth turns frantic in terror: both enemies brandish their swords and exit battling.

Malcolm and English soldiers capture Macbeth's army and seize his castle. Macduff announces that he has killed Macbeth. In a victory hymn, the soldiers rejoice that the tyrant is dead, destroyed by the wrath and fury of the Lord. Malcolm becomes King of Scotland, while on bended knee, all proclaim, "God save the King!"

Act I — Scene 1:
A forest. Three groups of witches appear amid thunder and lightning

Streghe:
Che faceste? dite su!
Ho sgozzato un verro. E tu?
M'è frullata nel pensier
La mogliera di un nocchier:
Al dimon la mi cacciò;
Ma lo sposo che salpò;
Col suo legno affogherò;
Un rovaio ti darò;
I marosi leverò;
Per le secche lo trarrò.

Witches:
What have you been doing? Tell us!
I have slit a boar's throat.
What have you done?
I'm thinking of a steersman's wife
who chased me to the devil,
but when her husband sets sail
I'll drown him with his ship.
I'll call for the north wind.
I'll raise the waves.
I'll drag it across the shallows.

Drumming is heard

Un tamburo! Che sarò?
Vien Macbetto. Eccolo qua!

A drum! What can it be?
Macbeth is coming. He is here.

Witches dance in a circle

Le sorelle vagabonde
van per l'aria, van sull'onde,
Sanno un circolo intrecciar
Che comprende e terra e mar.

The wandering sisters
Fly through the air, sail over the waves,
they bind a circle
through land and sea.

Act I — Scene 2
Macbeth and Banquo appear

Macbeth:
Giorno non vidi mai sì fiero e bello!

Macbeth:
I have never seen a day so fine and fierce!

Banco:
N'è tanto glorioso!

Banquo:
Nor so glorious!

Macbeth:
Oh, chi saranno costor?

Macbeth: *(noticing the witches)*
Oh, who are they?

Banco:
Chi siete voi? Di questo mondo
O d'altra regione?

Banquo:
Who are you? Are you from this world
or from some also place?

Dirvi donne vorrei, ma lo mi vieta
Quella sordida barba.

I should call you women, but your filthy
beards prevent me.

Macbeth:
Or via, parlate!

Macbeth:
Come, speak!

Streghe:
Salve, o Macbetto, di Glamis sire!
Salve, o Macbetto, di Caudor sire!
Salve, o Macbetto, di Scozia re!

Witches:
Hail, Macbeth, Thane of Glamis!
Hail, Macbeth, Thane of Cawdor!
Hail, Macbeth, King of Scotland!
(Macbeth trembles)

Banco:
Tremar vi fanno così lieti auguri?

Favellate a me pur, se non v'è scuro,
Creature fantastiche, il futuro.

Banquo: *(whispering to Macbeth)*
Do these happy prophecies make you
tremble? *(and then to the witches)*
Tell me as well about my future,
weird beings, if you can see it.

Streghe:
Salve!
Salve!
Salve!

Witches:
Hail!
Hail!
Hail!

Men sarai di Macbetto eppur maggiore!
Non quanto lui, ma più; di lui felice!
Non re, ma di monarchi genitore!

You will be lesser than Macbeth and yet
greater! Not so happy as he, but happier!
Not king, but the father of kings!

Tutte:
Macbetto e Banco vivano!
Banco e Macbetto vivano!

All: *(as the witches disappear)*
Long live Macbeth and Banquo!
Long live Banquo and Macbeth!

Macbeth:
Vanir!
Saranno i figli tuoi sovrani.

Macbeth: *(in deep thought)*
They have vanished!
They said your children will be kings.

Banco:
E tu re pria di loro.

Banquo:
And you will be king before them.

Banco e Macbeth:
Accenti arcani!

Banquo and Macbeth:
Mysterious thoughts!

Act I — Scene 3
The King's messengers arrive

Messaggeri:
Pro Macbetto! Il tuo signore
Sir t'elesse di Caudore.

Messengers:
Brave Macbeth, your lord
has made you Thane of Cawdor.

Macbeth:
Ma quel sire ancor vi regge!

Macbeth:
But that Thane is still living!

Messaggeri:
No! Percosso dalla legge
Sotto il ceppo egli spirò.

Messengers:
No! He has died on the block, struck down
by the law.

Banco:
Ah, l'inferno il ver parlò!

Banquo: *(aside)*
Ah, the devil spoke the truth!

Macbeth:

Due vaticini compiuti or sono.
Mi si promette dal terzo un trono.
Ma perchè sento rizzarmi il crine?
Pensier di sangue, d'onde sei nato?
Alla corona che m'offre il fato
La man rapace non alzerò.

Macbeth:

Prophetic visions of a crown now possess
me. But why do I feel my hair standing on
end?
Where have these thoughts of blood come
from? Fate offers me a crown which I will
not stretch out my hand to snatch.

Andante assai sostenuto
MACBETH

Due vati-ci - ni compiuti or sono   mi si pro-mette dal ter - so un trono...

Banco:
Oh, come s'empie costui d'orgoglio,
Nella speranza di un regio soglio!
Ma spesso l'empio Spirto d'averno
Parla, e c'inganna, veraci detti,
E ne abbandona poi maledetti
Su quell'abisso che ci scavò.

Banquo: *(aside)*
Oh, how the hope of a kingdom
fills him with pride!
But often the wicked spirit of hell
betrays us,
and we are cursed and abandoned,
standing above that abyss awaiting us.

Messaggeri:
Perchè si freddo n'udò; Macbetto?
perchè l'aspetto non serenò?

Messengers:
Why has Macbeth taken this news so
coldly? Why does he show no pleasure?

All depart, except the Witches

Act I — Scene 4
The witches return

Streghe:	**Witches:**
S'allontanarono! N'accozzeremo	They have gone! We shall come together
Quando di fulmini lo scroscio udremo.	again when we hear the crash of thunder.
S'allontanarono, fuggiam! s'attenda	They have gone. Let us go. We await
Le sorti a compiere nella tregenda.	destiny's fulfilment amid the
Macbetto ridere vedrem colò;	witches'sabbath. Macbeth will return, we
E il nostro oracolo gli parlerò;	shall see him there and our oracle will speak
Fuggiam, fuggiam!	to him. Let us go!

Act I — Scene 5
A hall in Macbeth's castle; Lady Macbeth reads a letter

Lady Macbeth:	**Lady Macbeth:**
"Nel dì della vittoria io le incontrai.	I met them on the day of victory.
Stupito io n'era per le udite cose;	I was stunned at what I heard;
Quando i nunzi del Re mi salutaro	when the King's messengers hailed me
Sir di Caudore, vaticinio uscito	Thane of Cawdor, it fulfilled a prophecy
Dalle veggenti stesse	those seers had made.
Che predissero un serto al capo mio.	They also predicted a crown for my head.
Racchiudi in cor questo segreto. Addio."	Keep this secret in your heart. Farewell."
Ambizioso spirto	You are an ambitious soul, Macbeth.
Tu sei Macbetto. Alla grandezza aneli,	You long for greatness,
Ma sarai tu malvagio?	but will you be wicked enough?
Pien di misfatti è il calle	The road to power is filled with crimes, and
Della potenza, e mal per lui che il piede	woe to him who sets an uncertain foot upon
Dubitoso vi pone, e retrocede!	it and retreats!

Andantino
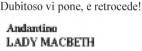

Vieni! t'affretta! Accen - dere   ti vo' quel freddo co - re!
Come! Hurry home! Kindle the desires in your cold heart!

Vieni t'affretta! Accendere	Come! Hurry home! Kindle the desires in
Ti vo' quel freddo core!	your cold heart!
L'audace impresa a compiere	I shall give you the courage
Io ti darò valore;	to carry out this bold undertaking.
Di Scozia a te promettono	The prophetesses promise you
Le profetesse il trono.	the throne of Scotland.
Che tardi? Accetta il dono,	Why delay? Accept the gift,
Ascendivi a regna.	mount the throne and reign.

Act I — Scene 6
A servant enters

Servo:
Al cader della sera il Re qui giunge.

Servant:
The King will come here this evening.

Lady Macbeth:
Che dì? Macbetto è seco?

Lady Macbeth:
What? Is Macbeth with him?

Servo:
È l'accompagna.
La nuova, o donna, è certa.

Servant:
He is accompanying him.
My lady, the news is certain.

Lady Macbeth:
Trovi accoglienza quale un re si merta.

Lady Macbeth:
Let him find a reception which is deserving
of a king.

The servant departs

Act I — Scene 7
Lady Macbeth alone

Lady Macbeth:
Duncano sarò qui?
Qui? Qui la notte?

Lady Macbeth:
Duncan will be here?
Here? Spend the night here?

Allegro maestoso
LADY MACBETH

Or tut - ti sorge - te, mini - stri inferna - li, che al sangue incorate,

Or tutti sorgete,
ministri infernali,
Che al sangue incorate,
spingete i mortali!
Tu, notte, ne avvolgi
di tenebre immota.
Qual petto percota
non vegga il pugnal.

Arise, all the
agents of hell
that rouse mortals
to bloody acts!
Night, wrap us
In motionless darkness.
Do not let the knife see
The breast which it strikes.

Act I — Scene 8
Lady Macbeth, alone with Macbeth

Macbeth:
Oh donna mia!

Macbeth:
Oh, my lady!

Lady Macbeth:
Caudore!

Lady Macbeth:
Cawdor!

Macbeth:
Fra poco il re vedrai.

Macbeth:
Soon you will see the King.

Lady Macbeth:
E partirò?

Lady Macbeth:
And when will he leave?

Macbeth:
Domani.

Macbeth:
Tomorrow.

Lady Macbeth:
Mai non ci rechi il sole un tal domani.

Lady Macbeth:
May the sun never bring that tomorrow.

Macbeth:
Che parli?

Macbeth:
What are you saying?

Lady Macbeth:
E non intendi?

Lady Macbeth:
Don't you understand?

Macbeth:
Inendo, intendo!

Macbeth:
I understand!

Lady Macbeth:
Or bene?

Lady Macbeth:
Well?

Macbeth:
E se fallisse il colpo?

Macbeth:
And if the blow should fail?

Lady Macbeth:
Non fallirò agrave; se tu non tremi,

Il Re!
Lieto or lo vieni ad incontrar con me.

Lady Macbeth:
It will not fail if you do not waver.
(Sounds of celebration are heard)
The King!
Come with me and greet him cheerfully.
(They depart)

Act I — Scene 9
In the castle.
Sounds of music are heard coming nearer, announcing the arrival of the king. Duncan
crosses the hall accompanied by Banquo, Macduff, Macbeth, Lady Macbeth and courtiers.

Act I — Scene 10
Macbeth speaks to a servant

Macbeth:
Sappia la sposa mia che, pronta appena
La mia tazza notturna,
Vo' che un tocco di squilla a me lo avvisi.

Macbeth:
Tell my wife that as soon as my night drink
is ready,
I wish to be alerted by a bell.
(The servant departs)

Act I — Scene 11
Macbeth alone

Macbeth:
Mi si affaccia un pugnal!
L'elsa a me volta?
Se larva non dei tu, ch'io ti brandisca.
Mi sfuggi, eppur ti veggo!

A me precorri
Sul conuso cammin che nella mente
Di seguir disegnava!
Orrenda imago!
Solco sanguigno la tua lama irriga!
Ma nulla esiste ancor. Il sol cruento
Mio pensier la diò forma, e come vera
Mi presenta allo sguardo una chimera.
Sulla metò del mondo

Or morta è la natura; or l'assasino
Come fantasma per l'ombre si striscia,
Or consuman le streghe i lor misteri,
Immobil terra!
a passi miei sta muta.

Macbeth:
Is this a dagger I see before me?
The hilt turned to me?
If you are not a dream, let me grasp you.
You fly from me, and yet I can see you!

You run ahead of me
along the unclear path which my mind
intended to follow!
Horrid sight!
The blade is streaked with blood!
But now there's nothing there.
Only my bloody imagination gives it shape
and presents a dream to my eyes as a
reality.

On one half of the world
nature now is dead. Now the murderer
creeps like a phantom through the shadows.
Now the witches consummate their secrets.
Motionless earth! Stay hushed at my steps.

A bell rings

È deciso.
quel bronzo, ecco, m'invita!
Non udirlo, Duncano!
È squillo eterno
Che nel cielo
ti chiama o nell'inferno.

It is decided.
That bell invites me!
Do not hear it, Duncan.
It is a knell
That summons you
to heaven or to hell.

Macbeth entersthe King's chambers

Act I — Scene 12
Lady Macbeth alone

Lady Macbeth:
Regna il sonno su tutti.
Oh, qual lamento!
Risponde il gufo
al suo lugubre addio!

Lady Macbeth:
Sleep reigns over everyone.
Ah, that moaning!
The owl responds
To his mournful farewell.

Macbeth:
Chi v'ha?

Macbeth: *(from inside)*
Who's there?

Lady Macbeth:
Ch'è fosse di letargo uscito
Pria del colpo mortal?

Lady Macbeth:
What if he was roused from his sleep
before the fatal blow?

Act I — Scene 13
Macbeth enters, his face contorted. He holds a bloodied dagger.

Macbeth:
Tutto è finito!

Fatal mia donna! un murmure,
Com'io non intendesti?

Macbeth:
It is all over.
(In a whisper to Lady Macbeth)
My fated lady, did you not hear
murmuring, as I did?

Lady Macbeth:
Del gufo udii lo stridere.
Che mai dicesti?

Lady Macbeth:
I heard the shriek of an owl.
What did you say a moment ago?

Macbeth:
Io?

Macbeth:
I?

Lady Macbeth:
Dianzi udirti parvemi.

Lady Macbeth:
I thought I heard you just now.

Macbeth:
Mentre io scendea?

Macbeth:
While I was coming down?

Lady Macbeth:
Sì! sì!

Lady Macbeth:
Yes!

Macbeth:
Dì nella stanza attigua
Chi dorme?

Macbeth:
Tell me, who is sleeping
in the side room?

Lady Macbeth:
Il regal figlio.

Lady Macbeth:
The King's son.

Macbeth:
O vista, o vista orribile!

Lady Macbeth:
Storna da questo il ciglio.

Macbeth:
Nel sonno udiò che oravano
I cortigiani,
Dio sempre ne assista, ei dissero;
Amen dir volli anch'io,
Ma la parola indocile
Gelò sui labbri miei.

Lady Macbeth:
Follie!

Macbeth:
Perchè ripetere
Quell'Amen non potei?

Lady Macbeth:
Follie, follie che sperdono
I primi rai del dì.

Macbeth:
Allora questa voce m'intesi nel petto:
Avrai per guanciali sol vepri, o Macbetto!
Il sonno per sempre, Glamis, uccidesti!
Non v'è che vigilia, Caudore, per te!

Lady Macbeth:
Ma dimmi, altra voce non parti d'udire?
Sei vano, o Macbetto, ma privo d'ardire:
Glamis, a mezz'opra vacilli, t'arresti,
Fanciul vanitoso, Caudore, tu sei.

Macbeth:
Vendetta! tuonarmi com'angeli d'ira,
Udiò Duncano le sante virtù.

Lady Macbeth:
Quell'animo trema, combatte, delira.
Chi mai lo direbbe l'invito che fu?
Il pugnal là riportate.

Macbeth: *(looking at his hands)*
Oh, what an awful sight!

Lady Macbeth:
Look away.

Macbeth:
I heard the courtiers
praying in their sleep.
God be with us always, they said.
I wanted to say Amen
but the rebellious word
froze on my lips.

Lady Macbeth:
Madness!

Macbeth:
Why could I not
say that Amen?

Lady Macbeth:
Such foolishness, but the first light of day:
will dispel it.

Macbeth:
Then I heard a voice within me saying:
O Macbeth, you will have only thorns for a
pillow. Glamis, you have murdered sleep
for ever. Cawdor will never sleep again.

Lady Macbeth:
But tell me, did you not hear another voice?
You are bold, Macbeth, but have no daring.
You hesitate halfway, Glamis, and stop.
Cawdor, you are a conceited child.

Macbeth:
I shall hear Duncan's holy virtues
thunder vengeance at me like angels of wrath.

Lady Macbeth:
His spirit is trembling, struggling and raving.
Who would ever call him the unconquered
man he was? Take the knife back there.

Le sue guardie insanguinate.
Che l'accusa in lor ricada.

Smear his guards with blood
so that they will be accused.

Macbeth:
Io colà? non posso entrar!

Macbeth:
I go there? I cannot go back in!

Lady Macbeth:
Dammi il ferro.

Lady Macbeth:
Give me the knife.

Act I — Scene 14
Lady Macbeth takes the dagger from Macbeth and enters the King's chambers

Act I — Scene 15
Macbeth alone. There is a loud knocking at the castle gate.

Macbeth:
Ogni rumore mi spaventa!

Oh! Questa mano!
Non potrebbe l'Oceano
Queste mani a me lavar!

Macbeth:
Every noise alarms me!
(Looking at his hands)
Oh, this hand!
The ocean could not
wash my hands clean!

Lady Macbeth and others enter

Lady Macbeth:
Ve'! le mani ho lorde anch'io;
Poco spruzzo, e monde son.
L'opra anch'essa andrò in oblio.

Lady Macbeth:
See! My hands are stained too.
A sprinkle of water and they will be clean
again. The deed too will pass into oblivion.
(The knocking continues)

Macbeth:
Odi tu? raddoppia il suon!

Macbeth:
Do you hear? They're knocking louder.

Lady Macbeth:
Vieni altrove! ogni sospetto
Rimoviam dall'uccisor;
Torna in te! fa cor, Macbetto!
Non ti vinca un vil timor.

Lady Macbeth:
Come away! We must remove
all suspicion from the murderer.
Be yourself, Macbeth. Have courage!
Don't be defeated by fear.

Macbeth:
Oh, potessi il mio delitto
Dalla mente cancellar!
Deh, sapessi, o Re trafitto,
L'alto sonno a te spezzar!

Macbeth:
Oh, if only I could wipe my crime
from my mind!
O murdered King, if only I could
rouse you from your deep sleep.

Lady Macbeth drags him off

Act I — Scene 16
Macduff and Banquo arrive

Macduff:
Di destarlo per tempo il Re m'impose:
E di già tarda è l'ora.
Qui m'attendete, o Banco.

Macduff:
The King ordered me to awaken him early,
and it is already late.
Wait here for me, Banquo.

Macduff enters the King's chamber

Act I — Scene 17
Banquo alone

Banco:
Oh, qual orrenda notte!
Per l'aer cieco lamentose voci,
Voci s'udian di morte.
Gemea cupo l'augel de' tristi auguri,
E della terra si sentì il tremore.

Banquo:
Oh what an awful night!
Mourning voices were heard
in the blind air, voices of death.
The bird of ill omen moaned gloomily
and the earth was felt to shake.

Act I — Scene 18
Macduff and Banquo

Macduff:
Orrore! orrore! orrore!

Macduff: *(appalled and agitated)*
Horror! Horror! Horror!

Banco:
Che avvenne mai?

Banquo:
What has happened?

Macduff:
Là dentro
Contemplate voi stesso.
io dir nol posso!

Macduff:
In there,
see for yourself.
I cannot say it!

Banquo rushes into the King's chamber

Correte! olà!
Tutti accorrete! tutti!

Hurry! Ho there!
Everyone come here!

Act I — Scene 19
Macbeth, Lady Macbeth, a Gentlewoman, Malcolm and servants

Oh delitto! oh delitto!
oh tradimento!

Murder! Murder!
Treason!

Lady Macbeth:
Qual subito scompiglio!

Lady Macbeth:
What sudden confusion!

Banco:
Oh noi perduti!

Banquo: *(stunned as he returns)*
We are lost!

Tutti:
Che fu? parlate!
che seguì di strano?

All:
What is it? Speak!
What has happened?

Banco:
È morto assassinato il Re Duncano!

Banquo: *(shocked)*
King Duncan has been murdered!

Tutti:
Schiudi, inferno, la bocca ed inghiotti
Nel tuo grembo l'intero creato;
Sull'ignoto assassino esecrato
Le tue fiamme discendano, o Ciel.

All:
Open your mouth, hell
and absorb all creation in your womb.
Heaven, let your flames fall
on the unknown, detestable murderer.

O gran Dio, che ne' cuori penetri,
Tu ne assisti, in te solo fidiamo;
Da te lume, consiglio cerchiamo
A squarciar delle tenebre il vel!

God, we trust in you alone, you can look
into our hearts, and help aid us.
We look to you for light and counsel
in order to pierce the veil of darkness.

L'ira tua formidabile e pronta
Colga l'empio, o fatal punitor;
E vi stampi sul volto l'impronta
Che stampasti sul primo uccisor.

Deadly castigator let your formidable,
ready anger take the villain
and mark his head as you marked
that of the first murderer.

END of ACT I

Act II - Scene 1
A room in Macbeth's castle. Macbeth enters; he is in deep thought

Lady Macbeth:
Perchè mi sfuggi, e fiso
Ognor ti veggo in un pensier profondo?
Il fatto è irreparabile! Veraci
Parlar le maliarde, e re tu sei.
Il figlio di Duncan, per l'improvvisa
Sua fuga in Inghilterra,
Parricida fu detto, e vuoto il soglio
A te lasciò.

Lady Macbeth:
Why are you avoiding me, and why
are you always so deep in thought?
The deed cannot he undone. The sorceresses
spoke the truth and you are king.
Because of his sudden flight to England
Duncan's son has been accused
of patricide and the throne
was left empty for you.

Macbeth:
Ma le spirtali donne
Banco padre di regi han profetato.
Dunque i suoi figli regneran? Duncano
Per costor sarò spento?

Macbeth:
But the witches predicted
that Banquo would father kings.
So will his sons reign?
Will Duncan have died for them?

Lady Macbeth:
Egli e suo figlio vivono, è ver.

Lady Macbeth:
He and his son are alive, it is true.

Macbeth:
Ma vita immortale non hanno.

Macbeth:
But they are not immortal.

Lady Macbeth:
Ah sì, non l'hanno!

Lady Macbeth:
No, they are not!

Macbeth:
Forz'è che scorra un altro sangue, o donna!

Macbeth:
My lady, more blood must flow!

Lady Macbeth:
Dove? Quando?

Lady Macbeth:
Where? When?

Macbeth:
Al venir di questa notte.

Macbeth:
Tonight.

Lady Macbeth:
Immoto sarai tu nel tuo disegno?

Lady Macbeth:
Will you be firm in what you intend?

Macbeth:
Banco! l'eternità t'apre il suo regno.

Macbeth:
Banquo, eternity opens its realm to you.

Macbeth rushes out

Act II - Scene 2
Lady Macbeth, in deep thought

Lady Macbeth: **Lady Macbeth:**

La luce langue, il faro spegnesi
Ch'eterno corre per gli ampi cieli!
Notte desiata provvida veli
La man colpevole che ferirè.

Nuovo delitto! È necessario!
Compiersi debbe l'opra fatale.
Ai trapassati regnar non cale;
A loro un requiem, l'eternità.

O voluttà del soglio!
O scettro, alfin sei mio!
Ogni mortal desio
Tace e s'acqueta in te.
Cadrà fra poco esanime
Chi fu predetto re.

The light is fading, the beacon that eternally
crosses the wide sky has gone out.
O longed-for night, throw a veil
over the guilty murderous hand.

A new crime! It must be so!
The fatal deed must be done.
Power means nothing to the dead;
for them a requiem and eternity.

Oh, desire of the throne!
Oh, sceptre, at last you are mine!
Every living desire
is quieted and calmed in you.
The man who was prophesied king
will soon fall lifeless.

Act II - Scene 3
In a park, assassins plan their ambush

Coro di Sicari:
Chi v'impose unirvi a noi?
Fu Macbetto.
Ed a che far?
Deggiam Banco trucidar.
Quando? Dove?
Insiem con voi.
Con suo figlio ei qui verrà.
Rimanete, or bene sta.

Tutti:
Sparve il sol, la notte or regni
Scellerata, insanguinata.

Assassins:
Who commanded you to join us?
It was Macbeth.
To do what?
We are to slaughter Banquo.
When? Where?
Together with you.
He will come here with his son.
Stay. All is well.

All:
The sun has disappeared, now let night
reign, wicked and bloodstained.

Cieca notte, affretta e spegni
Ogni lume in terra e in ciel.
L'ora è presso! or n'occultiamo,
Nel silenzio lo aspettiamo.
Trema, o Banco! nel tuo fianco
Sta la punta del coltel!

Blind night, hurry to extinguish
all light on earth and in heaven.
The time is near, now let us hide.
We shall wait for him in silence.
Tremble, Banquo, the point of a dagger
is stuck in your side!

Act II - Scene 4
Banquo and Fleance enter

Banco:
Studia il passo, o mio figlio
usciam da queste tenebre
un senso ignoto nascer mi sento il petto,
Pien di tristo presagio e di sospetto.
Come dal ciel precipita.

L'ombra più sempre oscura!
In notte ugual trafissero
Duncano, il mio signor.
Mille affannose immagini
M'annunciano sventura,
E il mio pensiero ingombrano
Di larve e di terror.

Banquo:
Hurry, my son, let us escape
from these shadows.
I can feel an unknown sensation rising in
my heart, filled with sad foreboding and
suspicion.

How the gloom falls more and more darkly
from heaven!
It was on a night like this that they stabbed
my lord Duncan. A thousand feverish
images foretell misfortune to me
and cloud my thoughts
with phantoms and fears.

They leave. Banquo's voice is heard

Fuggi, mio figlio!oh tradimento!

Flee, my son, what betrayal!

Fleance crosses the scene pursued by one of the assassins

Act II - Scene 5
A magnificent hall with a table set for a banquet.
Macbeth, Lady Macbeth, her Gentlewoman, Macduff, Knights and Ladies.

Coro:
Salve, o Re!

Chorus:
Hail, King!

Macbeth:
Voi pur salvete, nobilissimi signori.

Macbeth:
Hail to you, most noble lords.

Coro:
Salve, o donna!

Coro:
Hail, madam!

Lady Macbeth:
Ricevete la mercè dei vostri onori.

Lady Macbeth:
Accept my thanks for your praise.

Macbeth:
Prenda ciascun l'orrevole
Seggio al suo grado eletto.
Pago son io d'accogliere
Tali ospiti a banchetto.
La mia consorte assidasi
Nel trono a lei sortito,
Ma pria le piaccia un brindisi
Sciogliere, a vostr'onor.

Macbeth:
Let everyone take his place
according to his rank.
I am pleased to greet
such guests at the banquet.
Let my consort take
her appointed place on the throne.
But first let her offer
a toast in your honour.

Lady Macbeth:
Al tuo regale invito
Son pronta, o mio signor.

Lady Macbeth:
I am ready to answer
your royal request, my lord.

Coro:
E tu ne udrai rispondere
Come ci detta il cor.

Chorus:
And you will hear our reply,
prompted by our hearts.

Lady Macbeth:

Allegretto
LADY MACBETH

Si col - mi il ca - lice di vi - no e - let - to...

Si colmi il calice
Di vino eletto;
Nasca il diletto,
Muoia il dolor.

Fill the cup
with the choicest wine.
Give life to pleasure
And death to sorrow.

Da noi s'involino
Gli odi e gli sdegni,
Folleggi e regni
Qui solo amor.

Let hate and scorn
fly from us
and let love alone
reign here.

Giustiamo il balsamo
D'ogni ferita,
Che nova vita
Ridona al cor.

Let us savour the balm
for every wound
which gives new life
to the heart.

Cacciam le torbide
Cure dal petto;
Nasca il diletto,
Muoia il dolor.

Let us cast dull care
from our hearts;
give life to pleasure
and death to sorrow.

Tutti:
Cacciam le torbide
Cure dal petto; Nasca il diletto,
Muoia il dolor. Hail, King!

All:
Let us cast dull care
from our hearts; give life to pleasure
and death to sorrow.

Act II - Scene 6
An assassin appears at a side door. Macbeth approaches him

Macbeth:
Tu di sangue hai brutto il volto.

Macbeth: *(whispering)*
You have blood on your face.

Sicario:
È di Banco.

Assassin:
It is Banquo's.

Macbeth:
Il vero ascolto?

Macbeth:
Is this the truth?

Sicario:
Si.

Assassin:
Yes.

Macbeth:
Ma il figlio?

Macbeth:
What about his son?

Sicario:
Ne sfuggi!

Assassin:
He fled!

Macbeth:
Cielo! e Banco?

Macbeth:
Heavens! But Banquo?

Sicario:
Egli morì.

Assassin:
He is dead.

Act II - Scene 7
Macbeth dismisses the assassin

Lady Macbeth:
Che ti scosta, o re mio sposo,
Dalla gioia del banchetto?

Lady Macbeth: *(approaching Macbeth)*
My royal husband, what has drawn you
away from the delights of the banquet?

Macbeth:
Banco falla! il valoroso
Chiuderebbe io serto eletto
A quant'avvi di più degno
Nell'intero nostro regno.

Macbeth:
Banquo is not here. That courageous man
who would complete the chosen circle
of the most worthy in all our kingdom.

Lady Macbeth:
Venir disse, e ci mancò.

Lady Macbeth:
He said he would be here but he has failed us.

Macbeth:
In sua vece io sederò.

Macbeth:
I shall sit in his place.

Macbeth proceeds to sit down, but Banquo's ghost, which only he can see, is in his place

Di voi chi ciò fece?

Which of you has done this?

Tutti:
Che parli?

All:
What?

Macbeth:
Non dirmi, non dirmi ch'io fossi!
Le ciocche cruente non scuotermi incontro.

Macbeth: *(to the ghost)*
Do not say that it was I!
Do not shake your bloody locks at me!

Tutti:
Macbetto è soffrente!
Partiamo.

All:
Macbeth is ill!
Let us go.

Lady Macbeth:
Restate! Gli è morbo fugace.
E un uomo voi siete?

Lady Macbeth:
Stay! His sickness is passing.
Are you a man? *(whispering Macbeth)*

Macbeth:
Lo sono, ed audace
S'io guardo tal cosa che
al dimone istesso.

Macbeth:
I am, and a bold man if I can
look at such a thing which might frighten
the devil himself.

(to the ghost)

Porrebbe spavento nol ravvisi?

There ... there ... can't you see it?

Oh, poi che le chiome scrollar t' è concesso,
Favella! il sepolcro può render gli uccisi?

Since you can nod your head,
tell me, can the dead return from the grave?
(The ghost vanishes)

Lady Macbeth:
Voi siete demente!

Lady Macbeth: *(softly, to Macbeth)*
You are mad!

Macbeth:
Quest'occhi l'han visto.

Macbeth:
I saw him with my own eyes.

Lady Macbeth:
Sedete, o mio sposo!
Ogni ospite è tristo.
Svegliate la gioia!

Lady Macbeth:
Sit down, my husband!
All our guests are unhappy.
Re-awaken enjoyment!

Macbeth:
Ciascun mi perdoni:
Il brindisi lieto di nuovo risuoni,
Nè Banco obliate,
che lungi è tuttor.

Macbeth:
Forgive me, everyone.
Let the cheering toast be sung again,
and let us not forget Banquo
who is not with us.

Lady Macbeth:
Sì colmi il calice
Di vino eletto;
Nasca il diletto,
Muoia il dolor.

Lady Macbeth:
Fill the cup
with choicest wine.
Give life to pleasure
and death to sorrow.

Da noi s'involino
Gli odi e gli sdegni,
Folleggi e regni
Qui solo amor.

Let hate and scorn
fly from us
and let love alone
reign here.

Giustiamo il balsamo
D'ogni ferita,
Che nova vita
Ridona al cor.

Let us savour the balm
for every wound
which gives new life
to the heart.

Vuotiam per l'inclito
Banco i bicchieri!
Fior de' guerrieri,
Di Scozia onor.

Let us empty our glasses
to illustrious Banquo!
The flower of warriors,
The pride of Scotland.

The ghost reappears

Macbeth:
Va, spirto d'abisso!
Spalanca una fossa,
O terra l'ingoia.
Fiammeggian quell'ossa!

Macbeth: *(to the ghost)*
Go, spirit of hell!
Earth, open a ditch
and swallow him.
Those bones are burning.

Quel sangue fumante
mi sbalza nel volto!
Quel guardo a me volto
trafiggemi il cor!

That steaming blood
sprays in my face!
That look turns to me
And pierces my heart!

Tutti:
Sventura! terrore!

All:
Oh misfortune! Terror!

Macbeth:
Quant'altri io pur oso!
Diventa pur tigre, leon minaccioso

Macbeth:
I am as daring as any man!
You may become a tiger, a threatening lion,

M'abbanca Macbetto tremar non vedrai,
Conoscer potrai s'io provi timor
Ma fuggi!
deh, fuggi, fantasma tremendo!

La vita riprendo!

you may snatch me, but you will not see
Macbeth tremble. I feel fear!
But leave me!
Leave me, awesome ghost!
(The ghost disappears)
I am coming back to life!

Lady Macbeth:
Spirto imbelle! il tuo spavento
Vane larve t'ha creato.
Il delitto è consumato:
Chi morò tornar non può.

Vergogna, signor!

Lady Macbeth:
Cowardly spirit! Your fright
has created idle phantoms.
The crime is done.
The dead cannot return.

Shame, my lord!

Macbeth:
Sangue a me quell'ombra chiede
E l'avrà, l'avrà lo giuro!
Il velame del futuro
Alle streghe squarcierò.

Macbeth:
That shadow demands blood from me,
and it will have it, I swear it will have it!
I shall go to the witches
and pierce the veil of the future.

Macduff:
Biechi arcani! s'abbandoni
Questa terra: or ch'ella è retta
Da una mano maledetta
Viver solo il reo vi può Da una mano mal.

Macduff:
Sinister mysteries! He has spoken
terrified by phantoms.
This land has become
a den of thieves.

Tutti:
Biechi arcani! sgomentato
Da fantasmi egli ha parlato!
Uno speco di ladroni
Questa terra diventò.

All:
Sinister mysteries! He has spoken,
and he is terrified by phantoms.
This land has become
a den of thieves.

END of ACT II

ACT III - Scene 1
A dark cave. A boiling cauldron. Thunder and lightning.

Streghe:
Tre volte miagola la gatta in fregola.
Tre volte l'upupa lamenta ed ulula.
Tre volte l'istrice guaisce al vento.

Witches:
Three times the cat has mewed in heat.
Three times the hoopoe mourned and wailed.
Three times the porcupine yelped to the wind.

Tutte:
Questo è il momento.
Su via! sollecite giriam la pentola,
Mesciamvi in circolo possenti intingoli:
Sirocchie, all'opera! l'acqua già fuma,
Crepita e spuma.

All:
This is the hour!
Come, let us dance quickly round the
cauldron and mix powerful brews in our
circle. Sisters, to work! The water is
steaming, crackling and bubbling.

Tu, rospo venefico
Che suggi l'aconito,
Tu, vepre, tu, radica
Sbarbata al crepuscolo
Va', cuoci e gorgoglia
Nel vaso infernal.

Poisonous toad,
which sucks wolfsbane,
thorn, root
plucked at twilight,
cook and bubble
in the devil's pot.

Tu, lingua di vipera,
Tu, pelo di nottola,
Tu, sangue di scimmia,
Tu, dente di bàtolo,
Va', bolli e t'avvoltola
Nel brodo infernal.

Tongue of viper,
hair of bat,
blood of monkey,
tooth of dog,
boil and be swallowed up
in the infernal brew.

Tu, dito d'un pargolo
Strozzato nel nascere.
Tu, labbro d'un Tartaro,
Tu, cuor d'un eretico,
Va' dentro, e consolida
La polta infernal.

Finger of child
strangled at birth,
lip of Tartar,
heart of heretic,
thicken the
hellish broth.

Tutte:
E voi, Spirti
Negri e candidi,
Rossi e ceruli,
Rimescete!
Voi che mescere
Ben sapete,
Rimescete! Rimescete!

All:
Boil! Boil!
Sprits,
black and white,
red and blue
blend together!
You who well know how,
blend together!

ACT III - Scene 2
Macbeth appears at the entrance of the cave

Macbeth:
Finchè appelli, silenti m'attendete.

Che fate voi, misteriose donne?

Macbeth: *(to his men)*
Be quiet, and wai till I call you.
(To the witches)
What are you doing, mysterious women?

Streghe:
Un'opra senza nome.

Witches:
A work with no name.

Macbeth:
Per quest'opra infernal io vi scongiuro!
Ch'io sappia il mio destin, se cielo e terra
Dovessero innovar l'antica guerra.

Macbeth:
In the name of the infernal I implore you, let
me know my destiny even if heaven and
earth must renew their ancient struggle.

Streghe:
Dalle incognite posse udire lo vuoi,
Cui ministre obbediam, ovver da noi?

Witches:
Do you wish to hear it from the unknown
powers: whom we obey, or from us?

Macbeth:
Evocatele pur, se del futuro
Mi possono chiarir l'enigma oscuro.

Macbeth:
I invoke them, if they can tell me
the dark secrets of the future.

Streghe:
Dalle basse e dall'alte regioni,
Spirti erranti, salite, scendete!

Witches:
Wandering spirits, arise from the depths,
descend from the heights.

There is a flash of lightning. A head wearing a helmet appears from out of the ground.

Macbeth:
Dimmi, o spirto...

Macbeth:
Tell me, spirit ...

Streghe:
T'ha letto nel cuore;
Taci, e n'odi le voci segrete.

Witches:
He has read what is in your heart
Stay quiet and hear his secret words.

Apparizione:
O Macbetto! Macbetto! Macbetto!
Da Macduff ti guarda prudente.

Macbeth:
Tu m'afforzi l'ascolto sospetto!
Solo un motto...

Streghe:
Richieste non vuole.
Ecco un altro di lui più possente.

Lightning: a bloodstained child appears.

Taci, e n'odi le occulte parole.

Apparizione:
O Macbetto! Macbetto! Macbetto!
Esser puoi sanguinario, feroce:
Nessun nato di donna ti nuoce.

Macbeth:
O Macduffo, tua vita perdono
No! morrai! sul regale mio petto
Doppio usbergo sarà la tua morte!

Thunder and lightning. A child appears wearing a crown and carrying a sapling.

Ma che avvisa quel lampo, quel tuono?
Un fanciullo col serto dei Re!

Streghe:
Taci, ed odi.

Apparizione:
Sta' d'animo forte:
Glorioso, invincibil sarai
Fin che il bosco di Birna vedrai
Ravviarsi, e venir con te.

Macbeth:
Lieto augurio! Per magica possa
Selva alcuna giammai non fu mossa.

Or mi dite: salire al mio soglio
La progenie di Banco dovrà?

Apparition:
O Macbeth! Macbeth! Macbeth!
Beware Macduff!

Macbeth:
You confirm my suspicions at what I have
heard! Just one word ...
(The apparition vanishes)

Witches:
He will not hear questions.
Here is another, more powerful.

Stay quiet and hear his mysterious words.

Apparition:
O Macbeth! Macbeth! Macbeth!
You may be bloody and fierce:
no man born of woman will harm you.
(Apparition disappears)

Macbeth:
O Macduff, I forgive you your life.
No, you will die. Your death
will be a double shield on my royal breast!

But what does this thunder and lightning
mean? A child with a king's crown!

Witches:
Be quiet and listen.

Apparition:
Be strong:
you will be glorious and invincible
until you see Birnam wood
come marching towards you.
(Apparition disappears)

Macbeth:
Oh, what a cheering prophecy!
No wood was ever moved by magic power.
(To the witches)
Now tell me: will the descendants
of Banquo ever mount the throne?

Streghe:
Non cercarlo!

Witches:
Do not ask!

Macbeth:
Lo voglio! lo voglio,
o su di voi la mia spada cadrà!

La caldaia è sparita! perchè?

Qual concento! Parlate! Che v'è?

Macbeth:
I must know!
Or else my sword will fall on you!
(the cauldron sinks into the ground)
The cauldron has disappeared! Why?
(music is heard)
What is this music? Speak! What is it?

Streghe:
Apparite!
Apparite!
Apparite!

Witches:
Appear!
Appear!
Appear!

Tutte:
Poi qual nebbia di nuovo sparite.

All:
Then like mist it vanishes again.

Eight kings pass by, one after the other. Lastly Banquo appears, a mirror in his hand

Macbeth:

Macbeth:

Fuggi, regal fantasima,
Che Banco a me rammenti!
La tua corona è folgore,
Gli occhi mi fai roventi!

Via, spaventosa immagine,
Che il crin di bende hai cinto!

Ed altri ancor ne sorgono?
Un terzo? un quarto? un quinto?
O mio terror! dell'ultimo
Splende uno specchio in mano.

E nuovi Re s'ttergano
Dentro al cristallo arcano
è Banco, ahi, vista orribile!

Macbeth:
Away, royal phantom! You remind me of
Banquo. Your crown is a bolt of lightning
burning my eyes.

Away, frightening vision,
your brow is wrapped in bands!

Are there more?
A third? A fourth? A fifth?
Oh, horror! The last one
is carrying a mirror.

And new kings are endorsed
within the crystal.
And Banquo, oh, awful sight,

Ridendo a me li addita?
Muori, fatal progenie!

You laugh while you point them out to me?
Die, you deadly offspring!

He draws his sword and strikes at the ghost. He stops and then addresses the Witches.

Ah, che non hai tu vita!

But you have no life! Oh, terror!

Vivran costor?

Will they live?

Streghe:
Vivranno.

Witches:
They will live.

Macbeth:
Oh me perduto!

Macbeth:
Oh, I am lost!

Macbeth faints

Streghe:
Ei svenne! Aerei spirti,
Ridonate la mente al Re svenuto!

Witches:
He has fainted. Spirits of the air bring the
unconscious King back to his senses.

ACT III - Scene 3
The Witches dance and sing around Macbeth

Coro:
Ondine e Silfidi
Dall'ali candide,
Su quella pallida
Fronte spirate.
Tessete il vortice
Carole armoniche,
E sensi ed anima
Gli confortate.

Chorus:
Nymphs and
white-winged sylphs,
blow upon
that pallid brow,
weave a whirl
of sweet songs
to comfort
his body and soul.

Witches and spirits disappear

ACT III - Scene 4
Lady Macbeth, Macbeth and Araldo

Macbeth:
Ove son io? Fuggiro! Oh, sia ne secoli
Maledetta quest'ora in sempiterno!

Macbeth:
Where am I? They have gone! Oh, may this
hour be eternally damned!

Araldo:
La regina

Herald:
The Queen!

Macbeth:
(Che?)

Macbeth:
(What is it?)

Lady Macbeth:
Vi trovo alfin! Che fate?

Macbeth:
Ancora le streghe interrogai.

Lady Macbeth:
E disser?

Macbeth:
Da Macduffo ti guarda.

Lady Macbeth:
Segui.

Macbeth:
Te non ucciderà nato da donna.

Lady Macbeth:
Segui.

Macbeth:
Invitto sarai finchè acute; la selva
Di Birna contro te non mova.

Lady Macbeth:
Segui.

Macbeth:
Ma pur di Banco apparvemi la stirpe
E regnerà!

Lady Macbeth:
Menzogna!
Morte e sterminio sull'iniqua razza!

Macbeth:
Sì morte! Di Macduffo arda la rocca!
Perano moglie e prole!

Lady Macbeth:
Di Banco il figlio di rinvenga, e muoia!

Macbeth:
Tutto il sangue si sperda a noi nemico!

Lady Macbeth: *(entering)*
At last, I find you! What were you doing?

Macbeth:
I have been questioning the witches again.

Lady Macbeth:
And what did they say?

Macbeth:
To beware Macduff.

Lady Macbeth:
What else?

Macbeth:
That no man born of woman will kill me.

Lady Macbeth:
What else?

Macbeth:
I shall be unconquered until Birnam wood
marches against me.

Lady Macbeth:
What else?

Macbeth:
Yet Banquo's line appeared to me,
and they will reign!

Lady Macbeth:
Lies! Death and destruction to that wicked
brood!

Macbeth:
Yes, death! Macduff's castle must burn!
His wife and children must perish!

Lady Macbeth:
Let Banquo's son be found and killed!

Macbeth:
All our enemies' blood will be spilled.

Lady Macbeth:
Or riconosco il tuo coraggio antico.

Lady Macbeth:
Now I see your old courage again.

Macbeth e Lady Macbeth:

Macbeth and Lady Macbeth:

Ora di morte e di vendetta,
Tuona, rimbomba per l'orbe intero,
Come assordante l'atro pensiero
Del cor le fibre tutte intronò.

Ora di morte, ormai t'affretta!
Incancellabile il fato ha scritto:
L'impresa compiere deve il delitto
Poichè col sangue si inaugurò.

Hour of death and vengeance,
thunder resound throughout the entire world,
bewildering, like the dark intention
that has shaken our hearts to their depths.

Come quickly, hour of death,
Fate's remorseless decree; that this business
will end with crime since it was begun with
blood. Vengeance!

END of ACT III

Act IV — Scene 1

At the border between Scotland and England; in the distance is Birnam wood. Macduff is downcast. He stands apart from Scottish refugees, men, women and children.

Coro:
Patria oppressa! il dolce nome
No, di madre aver non puoi,
Or che tutta a figli tuoi
Sei conversa in un avel.

D'orfanelli e di piangenti
Chi lo sposo e chi la prole
Al venir del nuovo Sole
S'alza un grido e fere il Ciel.

A quel grido il Ciel risponde
Quasi voglia impietosito
Propagar per l'infinito,
Patria oppressa, il tuo dolor.

Suona a morto ognor la squilla,
Ma nessuno audace è tanto
Che pur doni un vano pianto
A chi soffre ed a chi muor.

Macduff:
O figli, o figli miei! da quel tiranno
Tutti uccisi voi foste, e insieme con voi
La madre sventurata!

Ah, fra gli artigli
Di quel tigre io lasciai la madre e i figli?

Chorus:
Oppressed land of ours! You cannot have
the sweet name of mother
now that you have become a tomb
for your sons.

From orphans, from those who mourn,
some for husbands, some for children,
at each new dawn a cry goes up
to outrage heaven.

To that cry heaven replies
as if moved to pity,
oppressed land, it would
proclaim your grief for ever.

The bell tolls constantly for death
but no one is so bold
as to shed a vain tear
for the suffering and dying.

Macduff:
Oh my children! You have all been killed
by that tyrant, together with
your poor mother!

Ah, did I leave a mother and her children in
the clutches of that beast?

Ah, la paterna mano
Non vi fu scudo, o cari,
Dai perfidi sicari
Che a morte vi ferir!

Alas, a father's hand was not there
to shield you, my dear ones,
from the treacherous assassins
who put you to death.

E me fuggiasco, occulto,
Voi chiamavate invano,
Coll'ultimo singulto,
Coll'ultimo respir.

And in vain you called on me,
a fugitive, in hiding,
with your last gasp,
with your last breath.

Trammi al tiranno in faccia,
Signore! e s'è mi sfugge,
Possa a colui le braccia
Del tuo perdono aprir.

Lord, bring me face to face
with this tyrant, and if he escapes me
let your merciful arms
open to him.

Act IV — Scene 2

Drums sound. Malcolm enters leading a large force of English soldiers.

Malcolm:
Dove siam? che bosco è quello?

Malcolm:
Where are we? What wood is that?

Coro:
La foresta di Birnamo!

Chorus:
Birnam wood.

Malcolm:
Svelga ognuno, e porti un ramo,
Che lo asconda, innanzi a s'é.

Ti conforti la vendetta.

Malcolm:
Let every man break off a branch and carry
it in front of him to conceal himself.
(to Macduff)
Let vengeance comfort you.

Macduff:
Non l'avrò; di figli è privo!

Macduff:
I cannot have it. He has no children.

Malcolm:
Chi non odia il suol nativo
Prenda l'armi e segua me.

Malcolm:
Whoever does not hate the land of his birth
let him take up arms and follow me.

Tutti:
La patria tradita
Piangendo ne invita!
Fratelli! gli oppressi
Corriamo a salvar.

All:
Our betrayed homeland
calls us, in tears.
Brothers! Let us run
to rescue the oppressed!

Già l'ira divina
Sull'empio ruina;
Gli orribili eccessi
L'Eterno stancar.

The wrath of God
will destroy the villain.
God has grown tired
of his awful crimes.

Act IV — Scene 3

A hall in Macbeth's castle. Night. A doctor and Lady Macbeth's gentlewoman.

Medico:
Vegliammo invan due notti.

Doctor:
We have waited in vain for two nights.

Dama:
In questa apparirà.

Gentlewoman:
She will appear tonight.

Medico:
Di che parlava nel sonno suo?

Doctor:
What was she talking about in her sleep?

Dama:
Ridirlo non debbo a uom che viva.
Eccola!

Gentlewoman:
I must not repeat it to any living person.
Here she is!

Act IV — Scene 4
Lady Macbeth enters, holding a lamp

Medico:
Un lume recasi in man?

Doctor:
That lamp in her hand?

Dama:
La lampada che sempre si tiene accanto al letto.

Gentlewoman:
It is the lamp which she keeps always beside her bed.

Medico:
Oh, come gli occhi spalanca!

Doctor:
Oh, her eyes are wide open!

Dama:
E pur non vede.

Gentlewoman:
Yet she cannot see.

Lady Macbeth puts down the lamp; she rubs her hands as if trying to remove a stain

Medico:
Perchè sfrega le man?

Doctor:
Why is she rubbing her hands?

Dama:
Lavarsi crede!

Gentlewoman:
She thinks that she's washing them.

Lady Macbeth:

Lady Macbeth:

Una macchia è qui tuttora.
Via, ti dico, o maledetta!

There's still a spot here.
Away, I tell you, curse you!

Una, Due, gli è questa l'ora!
Tremi tu? non osi entrar?
Un guerrier così codardo?
Oh vergogna! orsù t'affretta!
Chi poteva in quel vegiardo
Tanto sangue immaginar?

One, two, it is time!
Are you shaking? Don't you dare go in?
A soldier and so cowardly?
Shame! Come on, hurry!
Who would have thought that there would
be so much blood in that old man?

Medico:
Che parlò?

Doctor:
What did she say?

Lady Macbeth:
Di Fiffe il Sire
Sposo e padre or or non era?
Che n'avvenne?

E mai pulire queste mani
io non saprò?

Lady Macbeth:
The Thane of Fife
was he not recently a husband and father?
What happened?
(she stares at her hands)
Shall I never be able
to clean these hands?

Dama e Medico:
Oh terror!

Gentlewoman and Doctor:
Oh, horror!

Lady Macbeth:
Di sangue umano
Sa qui sempre. Arabia intera
Rimondar sì piccol mano
Co' suoi balsami non può.
Oimè!

Lady Macbeth:
There's still human blood here.
The perfumes of all Arabia
could not clean
this little hand.
Alas!

Medico:
Geme?

Doctor:
Is she moaning?

Lady Macbeth:
I panni indossa
Della notte. Or via, ti sbratta!
Banco è spento, e dalla fossa
Chi morò non surse ancor.

Lady Macbeth:
Put on your
nightgown. Come on, wash yourself!
Banquo is dead and no-one
has ever come back from the grave.

Medico:
Questo ancor?

Doctor:
This too?

Lady Macbeth:
A letto, a letto.
Sfar non puoi la cosa fatta.
Batte alcuno! andiam, Macbetto,
Non t'accusi il tuo pallor.

Lady Macbeth:
To bed, to bed.
What's done cannot be undone.
Someone is knocking! Come on, Macbeth,
do not let your pallor accuse you.

Dama:
Ah, di lei pietà, Signor!

Gentlewoman:
Oh, horror! Lord, have mercy on her!

Act IV — Scene 5
Macbeth's castle

Macbeth:
Perfidi! All'anglo contro me v'unite!
Le potenze presaghe han profetato:
Esser puoi sanguinario, feroce;
Nessuno nato da donna ti nuoce.

No, non temo di voi, n'è del fanciullo
Che vi conduce! Raffermar sul trono
Questo assalto mi debbe,
O sbalzarmi per sempre. Eppur la vita
Sento nelle mie fibre inaridita!

Pietà, rispetto, amore,
Conforto ai dì cadenti,
Non spargeran d'un fiore
La tua canuta età.

N'è sul tuo regio sasso
Sperar soavi accenti:
Sol la bestemmia, ahi lasso!
La nenia tua sarà!

Grida interne:
Ella è morta!

Macbeth:
Qual gemito?

Macbeth:
Traitors! You have joined with the English
against me! The powers that prophecy have
foretold: "You may be bloody and fierce,
no man born of woman will harm you."

No. I am not afraid of you, nor of the boy
who leads you, This attack will
confirm my position on the throne
or push me fom it for ever. And yet
I feel life drying up in my veins!

Mercy, respect, love,
the comfort of declining years,
these will place no flowers
on your old age.

Nor should you hope
for kind words on your royal tomb:
only curses, alas,
will be your funeral hymn.

Voices inside:
She is dead!

Macbeth:
What is that crying?

Act IV — Scene 6
The gentlewoman rushes in

Dama:
È morta la Regina!

Macbeth:

La vita... che importa?...
È il racconto d'un povero idiota;
Vento e suono che nulla dinota!

Gentlewoman:
The Queen is dead!

Macbeth: *(with indifference)*

Life... What does it matter?
It is the tale of a poor fool:
wind and sound signifying nothing.

Act IV — Scene 7
Soldiers enter

Coro:
Sire! ah, Sire!

Chorus:
Sire!

Macbeth:
Che fu? quali nuove?

Macbeth:
What is it? What news?

Coro:
La foresta di Birna si muove!

Chorus:
Birnam wood is moving!

Macbeth:
M'hai deluso, presago infernale!
Qui l'usbergo, la spada, il pugnale!
Prodi, all'armi! La morte o la gloria.

Macbeth:
You have deceived me, hellish prophecy!
Bring my shield, my sword, my dagger!
My valiant men, to arms! Death or victory!

Coro:
Dunque all'armi! sì morte o vittoria.

Chorus:
To arms then! Death or victory!

Act IV — Scene 8
A vast plain surrounded by hills and woods.
In the background are English soldiers, advancing slowly,
carrying branches in front of them.

Macduff:
Via le fronde, e mano all'armi!
Mi seguite!

Macduff:
Throw away the branches and take up your
arms! Follow me!

Malcolm, Macduff and the soldiers depart

Tutti:
All'armi! all'armi!

All:
To arms!

Act IV — Scene 9
Macbeth enters, followed by Macduff

Macduff:
Carnefice de' figli miei, t'ho giunto.

Macduff:
I have you, butcher of my children!

Macbeth:
Fuggi! Nato di donna
Uccidermi non può.

Macbeth:
Away! No man born of woman
can kill me.

Macduff:
Nato non son; strappato
Fui dal seno materno.

Macduff:
I was not born. I was plucked
from my mother's womb.

Macbeth:
Cielo!

Macbeth:
Oh God!

Act IV — Scene 10
Macbeth and Macduff brandish their swords and battle desperately.

Coro:
Infausto giorno!
Preghiam pe' figli nostri!
Cessa il fragor!

Chorus:
Unhappy day!
Let us pray for our sons!
Te clash of arms has stopped.

Voci:
Vittoria!

Voices:
Victory!

Donne:
Vittoria!

Chorus of Women: *(joyfully)*
Victory!

Act IV — Scene 11
Malcolm enters, followed by English soldiers, bards and people

Malcolm:
Ove s' è fitto l'usurpator?

Malcolm:
Where has the usurper gone?

Macduff:
Colà da me trafitto.

Salve, o re!

Macduff:
He's there, run through by me.
(Bending a knee to the ground)
Hail King!

Coro:
Salve, o re!
Macbeth, Macbeth ov'è?
Dov'è l'usurpator?
D'un soffio il fulminò;
Il Dio della vittoria.

Chorus:
Hail King!
Where is Macbeth?
Where is the usurper?
The God of victory struck him down
with a breath.

(to Macduff)

Il prode eroe egli è grave;
Che spense il traditor!
La patria, il re salvò;
A lui onore e gloria.

He is a valiant hero
who killed the traitor.
He has saved our homeland and our King,
honour and glory to him!

Coro di Donne:
Salgan mie grazie a te,
Gran Dio vendicator;
A chi ne liberò;
Inni cantiam di gloria.

Chorus of Women:
My thanks rise to you,
great God of vengeance.
Let us sing hymns of glory
to our liberator.

Macduff:
S'affidi ognun al re
Ridato al nostro amor!

Macduff:
Let all place their trust in the King
who has been given back to our love.

L'aurora che spuntò;
Vi darà pace e gloria!

The new dawn
will bring you peace and glory!

Malcolm:
Confida, o Scozia, in me;
Fu spento l'oppressor!
La gioia eternerà;
Per noi di tal vittoria.

Malcolm:
Scotland, trust in me.
The tyrant is dead.
I shall make everlasting
the joy of such a victory.

END of OPERA

DICTIONARY OF OPERA AND MUSICAL TERMS

Accelerando - Play the music faster, but gradually.

Adagio - At a slow or gliding tempo, not as slow as largo, but not as fast as andante.

Agitato - Restless or agitated.

Allegro - At a brisk or lively tempo, faster than andante but not as fast as presto.

Andante - A moderately slow, easy-going tempo.

Appoggiatura - An extra or embellishing note preceding a main melodic note. Usually written as a note of smaller size, it shares the time value of the main note.

Arabesque - Flourishes or fancy patterns usually applying to vocal virtuosity.

Aria - A solo song usually structured in a formal pattern. Arias generally convey reflective and introspective thoughts rather than descriptive action.

Arietta - A shortened form of aria.

Arioso - A musical passage or composition having a mixture of free recitative and metrical song.

Arpeggio - Producing the tones of a chord in succession rather than simultaneously.

Atonal - Music that is not anchored in traditional musical tonality; it does not use the diatonic scale and has no keynote or tonal center.

Ballad opera - Eighteenth-century English opera consisting of spoken dialogue and music derived from popular ballad and folksong sources. The most famous is *The Beggar's Opera,* which is a satire of the Italian opera seria.

Bar - A vertical line across the stave that divides the music into measures.

Baritone - A male singing voice ranging between bass and tenor.

Baroque - A style of artistic expression prevalent in the 17th century that is marked by the use of complex forms, bold ornamentation, and florid decoration. The Baroque period extends from approximately 1600 to 1750 and includes the works of the original creators of modern opera, the Camerata, as well as the later works by Bach and Handel.

Bass - The lowest male voice, usually divided into categories such as:

> **Basso buffo** - A bass voice that specializes in comic roles: Dr. Bartolo in Rossini's *The Barber of Seville.*

> **Basso cantante** - A bass voice that demonstrates melodic singing quality: King Philip in Verdi's *Don Carlos.*

> **Basso profundo** - the deepest, most profound, or most dramatic of bass voices: Sarastro in Mozart's *The Magic Flute.*

Bel canto - Literally, "beautiful singing." It originated in Italian opera of the 17th and 18th centuries and stressed beautiful tones produced with ease, clarity, purity, and evenness, together with an agile vocal technique and virtuosity. Bel canto flourished in the first half of the 19th century in the works of Rossini, Bellini, and Donizetti.

Cabaletta - A lively, concluding portion of an aria or duet. The term is derived from the Italian word "cavallo," or horse: it metaphorically describes a horse galloping to the finish line.

Cadenza - A flourish or brilliant part of an aria (or concerto) commonly inserted just before a finale. It is usually performed without accompaniment.

Camerata - A gathering of Florentine writers and musicians between 1590 and 1600 who attempted to recreate what they believed was the ancient Greek theatrical synthesis of drama, music, and stage spectacle; their experimentation led to the creation of the early structural forms of modern opera.

Cantabile - An indication that the singer should sing sweetly.

Cantata - A choral piece generally containing Scriptural narrative texts: the *St. Matthew Passion* of Bach.

Cantilena - Literally, "little song." A lyrical melody meant to be played or sung "cantabile," or with sweetness and expression.

Canzone - A short, lyrical operatic song usually containing no narrative association with the drama but rather simply reflecting the character's state of mind: Cherubino's "Voi che sapete" in Mozart's *The Marriage of Figaro.*

Castrato - A young male singer who was surgically castrated to retain his treble voice.

Cavatina - A short aria popular in 18th and 19th century opera that usually heralded the entrance of a principal singer.

Classical Period - A period roughly between the Baroque and Romantic periods, the late 18th through the early 19th centuries. Stylistically, the music of the period stresses clarity, precision, and rigid structural forms.

Coda - A trailer added on by the composer after the music's natural conclusion. The coda serves as a formal closing to the piece.

Coloratura - Literally, "colored": it refers to a soprano singing in the bel canto tradition. It is a singing technique that requires great agility, virtuosity, embellishments and ornamentation: The Queen of the Night's aria, "Zum Leiden bin ich auserkoren," from Mozart's *The Magic Flute.*

Commedia dell'arte - A popular form of dramatic presentation originating in Renaissance Italy in which highly stylized characters were involved in comic plots involving mistaken identities and misunderstandings. Two of the standard characters were Harlequin and Colombine: The "play within a play" in Leoncavallo's *I Pagliacci.*

Comprimario - A singer who performs secondary character roles such as confidantes, servants, and messengers.

Continuo, Basso continuo - A bass part (as for a keyboard or stringed instrument) that was used especially in baroque ensemble music; it consists of an independent succession of bass notes that indicate the required chords and their appropriate harmonies. Also called *figured bass, thoroughbass.*

Contralto - The lowest female voice, derived from "contra" against, and "alto" voice; a voice between the tenor and mezzo-soprano.

Countertenor - A high male voice generally singing within the female high soprano ranges.

Counterpoint - The combination of two or more independent melodies into a single harmonic texture in which each retains its linear character. The most sophisticated form of counterpoint is the fugue form, in which from two to six melodies can be used; the voices are combined, each providing a variation on the basic theme but each retaining its relation to the whole.

Crescendo - A gradual increase in the volume of a musical passage.

Da capo - Literally, "from the top"; repeat. Early 17th-century da capo arias were in the form of A B A, with the second A section repeating the first, but with ornamentation.

Deus ex machina - Literally "god out of a machine." A dramatic technique in which a person or thing appears or is introduced suddenly and unexpectedly; it provides a contrived solution to an apparently insoluble dramatic difficulty.

Diatonic - A major or minor musical scale that comprises intervals of five whole steps and two half steps.

Diminuendo - Gradually becoming softer; the opposite of crescendo.

Dissonance - A mingling of discordant sounds that do not harmonize within the diatonic scale.

Diva - Literally, "goddess"; generally the term refers to a leading female opera star who either possesses, or pretends to possess, great rank.

Dominant - The fifth tone of the diatonic scale; in the key of C, the dominant is G.

Dramatic soprano or tenor - A voice that is powerful, possesses endurance, and is generally projected in a declamatory style.

Dramma giocoso - Literally, "amusing (or humorous) drama." An opera whose story combines both serious and comic elements: Mozart's *Don Giovanni*.

Falsetto - A lighter or "false" voice; an artificially-produced high singing voice that extends above the range of the full voice.

Fioritura - It., "flowering"; a flowering ornamentation or embellishment of the vocal line within an aria.

Forte, fortissimo - Forte (*f*) means loud; mezzo forte (*mf*) is fairly loud; fortissimo (*ff*) is even louder; additional *fff*'s indicate greater degrees of loudness.

Glissando - Literally, "gliding." A rapid sliding up or down the scale.

Grand opera - An opera in which there is no spoken dialogue and the entire text is set to music, frequently treating serious and tragic subjects. Grand opera flourished in France in the 19th century (Meyerbeer); the genre is epic in scale and combines spectacle, large choruses, scenery, and huge orchestras.

Heldentenor - A tenor with a powerful dramatic voice who possesses brilliant top notes and vocal stamina. Heldentenors are well suited to heroic (Wagnerian) roles: Lauritz Melchior in Wagner's *Tristan und Isolde*.

Imbroglio - Literally, "intrigue"; an operatic scene portraying chaos and confusion, with appropriate diverse melodies and rhythms.

Largo or larghetto - Largo indicates a very slow tempo, broad and with dignity. Larghetto is at a slightly faster tempo than largo.

Legato - Literally, "tied" or "bound"; successive tones that are connected smoothly. The opposite of legato is staccato (short and plucked tones.)

Leitmotif - Literally, "leading motive." A musical fragment characterizing a person, thing, feeling, or idea that provides associations when it recurs.

Libretto - Literally, "little book"; the text of an opera.

Lied - A German song; the plural is "lieder." Originally, a German art song of the late 18th century.

Lyric - A voice that is light and delicate.

Maestro - From the Italian "master"; a term of respect to conductors, composers, directors, and great musicians.

Melodrama - Words spoken over music. Melodrama appears in Beethoven's *Fidelio* and flourished during the late 19th century in the operas of Massenet (*Manon* and *Werther*).

Mezza voce - Literally, "medium voice"; singing with medium or half volume. It is sometimes intended as a vocal means to intensify emotion.

Mezzo-soprano - A woman's voice with a range between soprano and contralto.

Obbligato - An accompaniment to a solo or principal melody that is usually played by an important, single instrument.

Octave - A musical interval embracing eight diatonic degrees; from C to C is an octave.

Opera - Literally, "work"; a dramatic or comic play in which music is the primary vehicle that conveys its story.

Opera buffa - Italian comic opera that flourished during the bel canto era. Highlighting the opera buffa genre were buffo characters who were usually basses singing patter songs: Dr. Bartolo in Rossini's *The Barber of Seville*; Dr. Dulcamara in Donizetti's *The Elixir of Love.*

Opéra comique - A French opera characterized by spoken dialogue interspersed between the musical numbers, as opposed to grand opera in which there is no spoken dialogue. Opéra comique subjects can be either comic or tragic.

Operetta, or light opera - Operas that contain comic elements and generally a light romantic plot: Strauss's *Die Fledermaus*, Offenbach's *La Périchole*, and Lehar's *The Merry Widow.* In operettas, there is usually much spoken dialogue, dancing, practical jokes, and mistaken identities.

Oratorio - A lengthy choral work, usually of a religious nature and consisting chiefly of recitatives, arias, and choruses, but performed without action or scenery: Handel's *Messiah.*

Ornamentation - Extra embellishing notes—appoggiaturas, trills, roulades, or cadenzas—that enhance a melodic line.

Overture - The orchestral introduction to a musical dramatic work that sometimes incorporates musical themes within the work. Overtures are instrumental pieces that are generally performed independently of their respective operas in concert.

Parlando - Literally, "speaking"; the imitation of speech while singing, or singing that is almost speaking over the music. Parlando sections are usually short and have minimal orchestral accompaniment.

Patter song - A song with words that are rapidly and quickly delivered. Figaro's "Largo al factotum" in Rossini's *The Barber of Seville* is a patter song.

Pentatonic - A five-note scale. Pentatonic music is most prevalent in Far Eastern countries.

Piano - A performance indication for soft volume.

Pitch - The property of a musical tone that is determined by the frequency of the waves producing it.

Pizzicato - An indication that notes are to be played by plucking the strings instead of stroking the string with the bow.

Polyphony - Literally, "many voices." A style of musical composition in which two or more independent melodies are juxtaposed; counterpoint.

Polytonal - Several tonal schemes used simultaneously.

Portamento - A continuous gliding movement from one tone to another through all the intervening pitches.

Prelude - An orchestral introduction to an act or a whole opera that precedes the opening scene.

Presto, prestissimo - Vigorous, and with the utmost speed.

Prima donna - Literally, "first lady." The female star or principal singer in an opera cast or opera company.

Prologue - A piece sung before the curtain goes up on the opera proper: Tonio's Prologue in Leoncavallo's *I Pagliacci.*

Quaver - An eighth note.

Range - The span of tonal pitch of a particular voice: soprano, mezzo-soprano, contralto, tenor, baritone, and bass.

Recitative - A formal device used to advance the plot. It is usually sung in a rhythmically free vocal style that imitates the natural inflections of speech; it conveys the dialogue and narrative in operas and oratorios. *Secco*, or dry, recitative is accompanied by harpsichord and sometimes with other continuo instruments; *accompagnato* indicates that the recitative is accompanied by the orchestra.

Ritornello - A refrain, or short recurrent instrumental passage between elements of a vocal composition.

Romanza - A solo song that is usually sentimental; it is shorter and less complex than an aria and rarely deals with terror, rage, or anger.

Romantic Period - The Romantic period is usually considered to be between the early 19th and early 20th centuries. Romanticists found inspiration in nature and man. Von Weber's *Der Freischütz* and Beethoven's *Fidelio* (1805) are considered the first German Romantic operas; many of Verdi's operas as well as the early operas of Wagner are also considered Romantic operas.

Roulade - A florid, embellished melody sung to one syllable.

Rubato - An expressive technique, literally meaning "robbed"; it is a fluctuation of tempo within a musical phrase, often against a rhythmically steady accompaniment.

Secco - "Dry"; the type of accompaniment for recitative played by the harpsichord and sometimes continuo instruments.

Semitone - A half step, the smallest distance between two notes. In the key of C, the half steps are from E to F and from B to C.

Serial music - Music based on a series of tones in a chosen pattern without regard for traditional tonality.

Sforzando - Sudden loudness and force; it must stand out from the texture and be emphasized by an accent.

Singspiel - Literally, "song drama." Early German style of opera employing spoken dialogue between songs: Mozart's *The Magic Flute.*

Soprano - The highest range of the female voice ranging from lyric (light and graceful quality) to dramatic (fuller and heavier in tone).

Sotto voce - Literally, "below the voice"; sung softly between a whisper and a quiet conversational tone.

Soubrette - A soprano who sings supporting roles in comic opera: Adele in Strauss's *Die Fledermaus*; Despina in Mozart's *Così fan tutte.*

Spinto - From the Italian "spingere" (to push); a singer with lyric vocal qualities who "pushes" the voice to achieve heavier dramatic qualities.

Sprechstimme - Literally, "speaking voice." The singer half sings a note and half speaks; the declamation sounds like speaking but the duration of pitch makes it seem almost like singing.

Staccato - Short, clipped, detached, rapid articulation; the opposite of legato.

Stretto - Literally, "narrow." A concluding passage performed in a quick tempo to create a musical climax.

Strophe - Strophe is a rhythmic system of repeating lines. A musical setting of a strophic text is characterized by the repetition of the same music for all strophes.

Syncopation - A shifting of the beat forward or back from its usual place in the bar; a temporary displacement of the regular metrical accent in music caused typically by stressing the weak beat.

Supernumerary - A "super"; a performer with a non-singing and non-speaking role: "Spear-carrier."

Symphonic poem - A large orchestral work in one continuous movement, usually narrative or descriptive in character: Franz Liszt's *Les Preludes*; Richard Strauss's *Don Juan, Till Eulenspiegel,* and *Ein Heldenleben.*

Tempo - The speed at which music is performed.

Tenor - The highest natural male voice.

Tessitura - The usual range of a voice part.

Tonality - The organization of all the tones and harmonies of a piece of music in relation to a tonic (the first tone of its scale).

Tone poem - An orchestral piece with a program.

Tonic - The principal tone of the key in which a piece is written. C is the tonic of C major.

Trill - Two adjacent notes rapidly and repeatedly alternated.

Tutti - All together.

Twelve-tone - The twelve chromatic tones of the octave placed in a chosen fixed order and constituting, with some permitted permutations and derivations, the melodic and harmonic material of a serial musical piece. Each note of the chromatic scale is used as part of the melody before any other note is repeated.

Verismo - Literally "truth"; the artistic use of contemporary everyday material in preference to the heroic or legendary in opera. A movement particularly in Italian opera during the late 19th and early 20th centuries: Mascagni's *Cavalleria rusticana*.

Vibrato - A "vibration"; a slightly tremulous effect imparted to vocal or instrumental tone to enrich and intensify sound, and add warmth and expressiveness through slight and rapid variations in pitch.

Opera Journeys™ Mini Guide Series

Opera Journeys™ Libretto Series

Opera Classics Library™ Series

A History of Opera: Milestones and Metamorphoses

Puccini Companion: the Glorious Dozen

Mozart's da Ponte Operas

Fifty Timeless Opera Classics

PUCCINI COMPANION: THE GLORIOUS DOZEN

756-page Soft Cover volume

Each Puccini Chapter features:

COMPLETE LIBRETTO
Italian-English side-by-side

STORY NARRATIVE
with 100s of Music Highlight Examples

ANALYSIS AND COMMENTARY

Print or Ebook

A HISTORY of OPERA: MILESTONES and METAMORPHOSES

432 pages, soft cover / 21 chapters

featuring   **Over 250 music examples**

• A comprehensive survey of milestones in opera history
• All periods are analyzed in depth:
Baroque, Classical, Romantic, Bel Canto, Opera Buffa, German
Romanticism, Wagner and music drama, Verismo,
plus analyses of the "Tristan Chord," atonalism, minimalism...

Print or Ebook

OPERA JOURNEYS' COLLECTION: FIFTY TIMELESS OPERA CLASSICS

816-page Soft Cover volume

Print or EBook

*A collection of fifty·of the most popular operas
in the Opera Journeys Mini Guide Series,
each with Story Narrative and 100s of Music Examples,
PLUS insightful,in delpth commentary and analysis*

MOZART'S DA PONTE OPERAS:

Don Giovanni, The Marriage of Figaro, Così fan tutte

348-page <u>Soft or Hard Cover</u> Edition

Print or Ebook

***Mozart: Master of Musical Characterization;
Da Ponte: Ambassador of Italian Culture.***

*Featuring: Principal Characters, Brief Story Synopsis, Story Narrative,
Music Highlight Examples, and insightful in depth Commentary and
Analysis, PLUS a newly translated LIBRETTO of each opera
with Italian/English translation side-by-side.*

ORDER: Opera Journeys' Web Site www.operajourneys.com

OPERA JOURNEYS LIBRETTO SERIES

Print or Ebook

New translations (side-by-side) with Music Highlight Examples

•Aida •The Barber of Seville •La Bohème
•Carmen •Cavalleria Rusticana •La Cenerentola
•Così fan tutte •Don Carlo •Don Giovanni
•La Fanciulla del West •Gianni Schicchi
•Lucia di Lammermoor •Madama Butterfly
•The Magic Flute •Manon Lescaut
•The Marriage of Figaro •A Masked Ball
•Otello •I Pagliacci •Rigoletto •La Rondine
•Salome Samson and Delilah •Suor Angelica
•Il Tabarro •Tosca •La Traviata •Il Trovatore •Turandot

OPERA JOURNEYS MINI GUIDE SERIES

Print or Ebook

featuring 125 titles

• *Brief Story Synopsis*

• *Principal Characters*

• *Story Narrative*

• *Music Highlight Examples*

• *Commentary and Analysis*

•The Abduction from the Seraglio •Adriana Lecouvreur •L'Africaine •Aida •Andrea Chénier
•Anna Bolena •Ariadne auf Naxos •Armida •Attila •The Ballad of Baby Doe •The Barber of Seville
•Duke Bluebeard's Castle •La Bohème •Boris Godunov •Candide •Capriccio •Carmen
•Cavalleria Rusticana •Cendrillon •La Cenerentola •La Clemenza di Tito •Le Comte Ory
•Così fan tutte •The Crucible •La Damnation de Faust •The Death of Klinghoffer •Doctor Atomic
• Don Carlo • Don Giovanni •Don Pasquale •La Donna del Lago •The Elixir of Love •Elektra
•Ernani •Eugene Onegin •Exploring Wagner's Ring •Falstaff •La Fanciulla del West •Faust
•La Fille du Régiment •Fidelio •Die Fledermaus •The Flying Dutchman •Die Frau ohne Schatten
•Der Freischütz •Gianni Schicchi •La Gioconda •Hamlet •Hansel and Gretel •Henry VIII
•Iolanta •L'Italiana in Algeri •Les Huguenots •Iphigénie en Tauride •Julius Caesar •Lakmé
•Lohengrin •Lucia di Lammermoor •Macbeth •Madama Butterfly •The Magic Flute
•The Makropolis Case •Manon •Manon Lescaut •Maria Stuarda •The Marriage of Figaro
•A Masked Ball •Die Meistersinger •The Mikado •Nabucco •Nixon in China •Norma
•Of Mice and Men •Orfeo ed Euridice •Otello •I Pagliacci •Parsifal •The Pearl Fishers
•Pelléas et Mélisande •Porgy and Bess •Prince Igor •I Puritani •The Queen of Spades
•The Rake's Progress •The Rape of Lucretia •The Rhinegold •Rigoletto •The Ring of the Nibelung
•Roberto Devereaux •Rodalinda •Roméo et Juliette •La Rondine •Der Rosenkavalier •Rusalka
•Salome •Samson and Delilah •Show Boat •Siegfried •Simon Boccanegra •La Sonnambula
•Suor Angelica •Susannah •Il Tabarro •The Tales of Hoffmann •Tannhäuser •Thaïs •Tosca
•La Traviata •Tristan and Isolde •Il Trittico •Les Troyens •Il Trovatore •Turandot
•Twilight of the Gods •The Valkyrie •Werther •West Side Story •Wozzeck

ORDER: Opera Journeys' Web Site www.operajourneys.com

Made in United States
North Haven, CT
27 May 2022

19579534R00049